COLOUR DECORATION
OF ARCHITECTURE

LECTOR HOUSE PUBLIC DOMAIN WORKS

COLOUR DECORATION OF ARCHITECTURE

JAMES WARD

ISBN: 978-93-5614-206-0

Published: 1914

© 2022
LECTOR HOUSE LLP

LECTOR HOUSE LLP
E-MAIL: lectorpublishing@gmail.com

Plate 1.— Sketch Design for a Wall Decoration in Fresco. By Author.

Fame Rewarding the Arts and Sciences.

COLOUR DECORATION OF ARCHITECTURE

TREATING ON COLOUR AND DECORATION OF
THE INTERIORS AND EXTERIORS OF BUILDINGS.
WITH HISTORICAL NOTICES OF THE ART
AND PRACTICE OF COLOUR DECORATION IN ITALY,
FRANCE, GERMANY AND ENGLAND.
FOR THE USE OF DECORATORS AND STUDENTS

BY

JAMES WARD

AUTHOR OF "PRINCIPLES OF ORNAMENT," "HISTORIC ORNAMENT,"
"COLOUR HARMONY AND CONTRAST," "PROGRESSIVE
DESIGN," "FRESCO PAINTING," ETC.

WITH TWELVE ILLUSTRATIONS IN COLOUR
AND TWENTY-TWO IN HALF-TONE

1914

PREFACE

This book is written with the view that it may be of practical service to the decorator, student and craftsman, who may be engaged in the practice and art of colour decoration, as applied to the interiors and exteriors of public buildings, churches, and private dwellings. I trust also it will be of some value to all who take an interest in the decoration of their own houses. The people of our own countries have been so unaccustomed to coloured buildings for the last three or four hundred years that a strong prejudice against the use of colour in architecture has been developed and is maintained even at the present day. Though we may all love colour, there are very few amongst us who have the courage to advocate its use in the decoration of buildings. We visit Italy, France, Germany, and the East, and admire the many and beautifully decorated churches, palaces, city halls and other public and private buildings, but the lessons we may have learned are lost to us, for we come back to our country to still hug our ancient prejudice against the use of colour, and are contented with the greyness of life, and with the dreariness and drab of our great manufacturing cities.

It is fashionable just now for many of our educated classes to talk largely on art and decoration on public platforms, and to air their artistic views in newspapers and magazines, but when it comes to a question of the practical application of their preaching and writing, they are found wanting, their courage seems to evaporate, as they think they have done their duty in the advancement of art by simply talking about it. In the fourteenth and fifteenth centuries in England there was a school of living art, and five or six centuries previous there was one in Ireland. Is it too much to expect these golden ages of art to return to us? We hope not, but before they do, art must become a common thought with the people, which can hardly be said to be the case at present.

I have included in this work some brief historical reviews of colour decoration in Italy, France, Germany and England, not so much on historical lines, but in order to offer to the decorator and student some account of the styles, methods and practice of the art under consideration in the countries named, and in hopes that what I have written in respect to these matters may prove of practical value to the readers of this book.

I desire to thank the Authorities of the Victoria and Albert Museum, The Dublin National Museum, the Dean of St. Alban's Cathedral, and Mr. William Davidson, L.R.I.B.A., Architect, Edinburgh, for their kind permission to use the illustrations acknowledged to them in this work.

J. WARD.

CONTENTS

Chapter	*Page*
Preface	vi
I. Colour Decoration of Architecture — Introductory	1
II. The Value of Colour as Applied to Architecture	8
III. The Decorative Colouring of Interiors	12
IV. The Colouring of Exteriors	25
V. On the Use and Modification of Colour in Decoration	30
VI. Italian Decoration and Ornament	38
VII. Coloured Architecture in France	53
VIII. Colour Decoration in Germany	62
IX. Colour Decoration in England	75
Index	90

LIST OF ILLUSTRATIONS

Page

- Plate 1.—Sketch Design for a Wall Decoration in Fresco. By Author.. iv

- Plate 2.—Frescoes in the Chapel of St. Peter Martyr, Church of St. Eustorgio, Milan.. 4

- Plate 3.—Design in Colour for the Decoration of Park Green Church, Macclesfield. By Author.. 7

- Plate 4.—Saint Michael: From a Painting on the Rood Screen, Ranworth Church, Norfolk. English, Early Sixteenth Century. From Water-colour by W. Davidson. 10

- Plate 5.—Design in Colour for the Decoration of the Town Hall, Macclesfield. By Author. 13

- Plate 6.—Colour Arrangement for the Decoration of a Room. 15

- Plate 7.—Three Suggestions of Colour Tints for Painted Walls or Paperhangings, as Backgrounds for Framed Pictures. 16

- Plate 8.—Design in Colour for the Decoration of a Morning Room Ceiling at Queen's Gate, London. By Author.. 18

- Plate 9.—Decorated Mouldings: From the Rood Screen, Ranworth Church, Norfolk. English, Early Sixteenth Century. Drawn by W. Davidson.. 21

- Plate 10.—Design in Colour for a Frieze Decoration. By Author. 23

- Plate 11.—Colour Arrangements for Doors and Woodwork. 24

- Plate 12.—Mosaic Panel: From the Cartoon of the Mosaic in St. Paul's Cathedral, London: Melchizedek Blessing Abraham. By Sir W. B. Richmond, K.C.B., R.A. 34

- Plate 13.—Approximate Change in Certain Colours when seen in Artificial Light.. 37

- Plate 14.—Model of Chapel of St. Catherine in the Church of St. Maurizo, Milan. Victoria and Albert Museum. .39

- Plate 15.—Mosaic Decoration: Church of St. John Lateran, Rome. By Jacopo Torriti. 1287-1292. 40

- Plate 16.—Portion of the Ornament in Mosaic of the Window Reveals: Church of St. John Lateran, Rome: 1287-1292.. 41

- Plate 17.—Italian Gothic Decoration in the Church of St. Anastasia at Verona.. 44

- Plate 18.—Decoration of a Portion of one of the Rooms in the Macchiavelli Palace, Florence. From a Model in the Victoria and Albert Museum. . 45

- Plate 19.—Portion of a Coloured Ceiling (Coved-Ceiling) Decoration by Giulio Romano, in the Palazzo Vecchio at Mantua. Sixteenth Century. . 46

- Plate 20.—Arabesque Decorations in the Ducal Palace, Mantua. By Giulio Romano. Sixteenth Century.. 48

- Plate 21.—Coloured Decoration of Portion of a Coved Ceiling in the Vatican. By Raffaelle. Sixteenth Century. 50

- Plate 22.—Decoration of the Boudoir of Madame de Serilly, now in the Victoria and Albert Museum. French, Eighteenth Century.. 55

- Plate 23.—Another Portion of the Decoration of the Boudoir of Madame de Serilly: French, Eighteenth Century. 56

- Plate 24.—Decoration in Colour of a Groined Ceiling in the Church of St. Jacques, Liége, 1522-1588. 67

- Plate 25.—Example of Diaper Ornament, largely used in Italian, German and English Decoration of the Sixteenth Century. 69

- Plate 26.—Example of Diaper Pattern, used in Italian, German and English Decoration of the Sixteenth Century.. 73

- Plate 27.—Example of Diaper Ornament, used in Italian, German and English Decoration of the Sixteenth Century.. 74

- Plate 28.—Saint George. From the Rood Screen, Ranworth Church, Norfolk: Early Sixteenth Century. From a Water-colour by W. Davidson, Architect.. 79

- Plate 29.—Decorated Mouldings, from the Rood Screen, Marsham Church, Norfolk: English, Sixteenth Century. Drawn by W. Davidson. . . . 80

- Plate 30.—Decorated Mouldings, from the Rood Screen, Cawston Church, Norfolk: English, Early Sixteenth Century. Drawn by W. Davidson. 82

- Plate 31.—Portion of Ceiling Decoration, Choir of St. Albans Abbey. 83

- Plate 32.—Decoration on the Rood Screen, Ranworth Church, Norfolk: Early Sixteenth Century. Drawn by W. Davidson. 85

- Plate 33.—Portion of Room Decoration formerly existing at Sheen House, Surrey. Eighteenth Century. .88

- Plate 34.—Portion of Staircase Decoration in the Victoria and Albert Museum. By F. W. Moody. .89

COLOUR DECORATION OF ARCHITECTURE

CHAPTER I

COLOUR DECORATION OF ARCHITECTURE— INTRODUCTORY

"I cannot consider Architecture as in anywise perfect without Colour."

Ruskin: *Seven Lamps of Architecture.*

THE History of Art testifies, in all its great periods, to the keen delight that artists, decorators, and architects have taken in the study of colour, and its expression in certain harmonious proportions and arrangements for the decoration of buildings. Colour was obtained for the adornment of a building by the use of marbles, metals, enamelled bricks and floor mosaics, which may be classed as permanent colouring, and structural in character, or it was applied, as in painting, wall mosaics, and stained glass. Architects were not content with leaving their buildings in grey and drab, for in such periods of the past, no building was considered complete without its final application of colour decoration.

Nature, for the solace of mankind, has made most of her works beautiful, by dressing them in coloured garments. Birds, insects, stones, gems, trees, flowers and "weeds of glorious feature"; the countless phases of the earth, the sea, and the sky with its clouds, when rosy-fingered at the dawn, when sunlit in noon-day beauty, or when fringed with the gold and crimsoned fires of the dying day, afford the clearest evidence that nature delights in rich and bright, as well as in quiet schemes of colour harmony. Therefore, if true art is built on the solid ground of nature, colour cannot well be divorced from it, for although certain uncoloured artistic creations are legitimate enough, they come under the head of illustrations, or are portions of coloured schemes of decoration, for colourless art, like colourless nature, is almost a contradiction in terms.

Even a whitewashed wall, when left some time to the weather, will be eventually changed into a variegated surface having delicate tints or suggestions of almost every colour. We might also illustrate nature's dislike to monotonous uniformity of tone if we select any other colour, however brilliant or intense, instead of white. The doors and windows of a house may be painted, for example, in a uniform colour of the rankest and crudest green imaginable, but if left long enough to the effects of the weather, this harsh colour will be transformed to a beautiful and variegated harmony of numerous and closely related tones, varying perhaps from greys to emerald greens and peacock blues, or in other words the rank and uniform harshness of the original colour will be eventually oxidised and bleached into a colour harmony of variegated beauty.

From our knowledge of the changes in colour made by sunshine and storm on outside painting and on whitewash, it might be suggested that a country cottage with white walls should have the doors and other woodwork, such as window shutters and frames, painted in a strong and rich green, and the window sashes in vermilion. Such a cottage should have a roof of thatch, or failing that, a red-tiled roof. In a few months after the cottage was painted it would lose any supposed harshness of colour that it might have had when first done, and would afterwards present a pleasant note of subdued richness of colour, that would be in complete harmony with the country or landscape around it. But if the cottage must have a slate roof, and if its walls are of red brick, then the doors, window shutters and frames should still be painted green, slightly inclining to yellow, but the window sashes should be painted white.

As regards the outside painting of the modern "concrete" cottages and villas, which are now contributing so much to the deepening of the grey and gloom of town and country, nothing short of the addition of inlaid panels of mosaic, or tile decoration, and the most brilliant colours imaginable on the woodwork will serve to relieve the dreary and leaden-hued monotony of the Portland cement walls.

If we love to see colours in nature and in pictures, why should we not also love to see a beautiful, a commonplace, or even any badly designed building decorated in pleasant schemes of harmonious colouring? We are quite prepared to hear the modern critic, as well as the modern "cubist," reply to this, that "art is art because it is not nature," that "it is absurd for an artist to worship, or to represent Beauty," or they may use any other convenient shibboleth, to protest against the representation of nature in art either in form or colour.

The question may be asked, "Why are the outsides of our modern buildings practically colourless?" when we know that during the ancient, medieval, and the early Renaissance periods the exteriors, as well as the interiors of all buildings were strongly coloured, either by the means of using natural marbles, metal-work, tiles, mosaics, or by painted decorations. Many notable examples of colour decoration, both exterior and interior, it is true, have been executed in modern times, but modern nations are still very timid in the use of colour, especially in regard to its application to the exterior of buildings. We are not yet quite emancipated from the white, grey, or drab effects, but we must at least be thankful for the note of colour in the red brick, and occasional red-tiled roof of the modern dwelling-house.

Our lack of colour appreciation has generally been laid to the charge of Puritanism, but this has been hitherto chiefly associated with the white-washing of church interiors. Cromwell, or rather his fanatical followers, have had a deal to answer for as iconoclasts, but at the same time it must be remembered that Cromwell was a friend of artists, and a patron of the arts in his day, and we certainly are indebted to him for the preservation of Raffaelle's Cartoons, the masterpieces of that great painter, which he hid in safety in the cellars of Hampton Court Palace during the troubles of the Civil War. Since Cromwell's time, however, colour decoration has crept into many of our public buildings, and some buildings in England were treated in colour thirty or forty years ago; but to-day, and we can hardly blame Cromwell for this, figuratively speaking, it may be said that a fresh colour-destroying wave of whitewash is sweeping over the country, which is now blotting out the former efforts of our old decorators.

The interiors of most of our public buildings are generally of an indescribable drab colour, if they are not painted white. It requires some courage to decorate properly in colour, as well as experience and ability, but it is very humiliating to find that notwithstanding our plentiful supply of decorative artists, the majority of our public buildings are painted in the style which we find frequent in bathrooms. The white of the bathroom has certainly something to recommend it. It looks decidedly clean, when it is freshly done, and has an air of great humility. Many people advocate white because, they say, it is safe, that is, because it relieves them of the solving of a colour problem; some museum authorities recommend it because they say that it is the best contrasting background for the objects and examples. The palace and the ballroom people advocate it because they think that ladies' dresses and Court uniforms look best against it, but all these reasons are just the ones that an artist would put forward to prove that white is not the best background for museum objects, and should not be used for the walls of a state assembly-room.

Dark, or strongly coloured objects in a museum look doubly darker against white walls, so that often you cannot see the beauty of their forms or the modelling and colour value of their surface details unless you get your eye quite close to them, which is sometimes impossible. On the other hand, suitably coloured and decorated walls often bestow a certain charm on the objects and examples by enhancing their beauty and preciousness, and by linking them together with the decoration, avoiding that mechanical and cold effect of isolation which many objects present on the colourless and undecorated walls of some museums.

As regards ballrooms, or state assembly-rooms, white walls make the worst kind of backgrounds for dresses and uniforms, as they afford too great a contrast with brightly coloured ones, and in the case of white dresses no contrast at all.

There is evidently a strong objection to the use of colour for the decoration of our public buildings; it is avoided as if it were an unholy thing, something desperately wicked, like the "scarlet and purple" trappings of the unhallowed lady of Babylon. Yet we see that the Almighty has clothed His glorious creation in thousands of tints of lovely colours, and on the other hand we find that Nature uses white very sparingly indeed. We moderns, however, live an artificial life, we are always in such a hurry that we have neither time nor inclination to learn the lessons we should learn from Nature; and besides, we are more or less obsessed with a puritanical pride, like the pride which apes humility, so in our indifference to the beauty of colour we seek for salvation in whitewash and plenty of it.

[National Museum, Dublin.

**Plate 2.— Frescoes in the Chapel of St. Peter Martyr,
Church of St. Eustorgio, Milan.**

(From portion of the model in the National Museum, Dublin.)

Perhaps, however, the Italian architect, Palladio, who flourished in the sixteenth century, was really more responsible than Puritanism for the fashion of colourless buildings, for he was one of the first who regarded colour as an evil thing, as he has said that "white was more acceptable to the Gods," an absurd statement, if he believed that the Gods were responsible for the colouring of Nature. It may be safely stated that the fashion of colourless buildings had its inception in Europe in Palladio's time, for previous to this date, which ushered in the decadence of the Renaissance, all the interiors and exteriors of buildings were decorated in colour from the earliest historic times. Any ancient building that had any architectural pretensions was not only coloured, but treated in the richest and brightest colours known to the decorator, and such colours were applied in their full strength. In the present day we have got so much accustomed to the absence of colour in architecture that when we do see the rare example of a richly coloured interior—exterior colouring is out of the question—which is not often, we must admit, we may be shocked by the novelty of it, and though we may secretly admire the daring of the decorator, we should be accused of our bad taste if we ventured to give it our unqualified approval.

Much as we all love colour, we seem to be afraid to get too far away from white, or very pale and neutral tints, in decoration. We appear to be too timid, or anxious not to offend the Palladian taste of the public. On the other hand, in the matter, for example, of church decoration, we are extraordinarily inconsistent, for we tolerate and encourage the employment of the most daring combinations of colour in stained-glass windows, and yet, as a rule, leave the rest of the architecture colourless and cold, so that in the majority of our churches the walls and ceilings look more chilly and cheerless in contrast with the brilliant glories of their stained-glass windows. The majority of our churches are a kind of reflex of the present general aspect of many medieval ones that have had their former decoration sacrilegiously scraped off their piers, walls, ribs, and ceiling vaults, and so deprived of their former beauty and comeliness.

Architecture is the mother of the arts and crafts, and she certainly looks all the happier when accompanied by her children, Sculpture and Painting, but when they are absent from her, her dignity is not augmented or enhanced by her saddened expression of loneliness that accentuates the coldness of her isolation.

We suppose that no one objects to the fashion of filling church windows with coloured glass; on the contrary, we should be thankful that in these modern times this reminiscence of ancient colour expression still remains to us, but why do we draw the line at coloured windows? Why are we not more consistent, and colour also the rest of our churches, interiors and exteriors as well, with coloured marbles, mosaic, or painted decoration? Seeing that we tolerate and admire colour decoration in stained-glass windows, there seems to be no legitimate reason why we should not have panels of coloured mosaic, enamelled terra-cotta or tiles, fresco, or coloured marbles as vehicles of colour decoration in churches as well as stained glass. Any of these materials or methods of decorative colour expression might well be used in the carrying out of designs for memorials of our departed friends, and would be quite as effective for such purposes as stained glass. But who has ever seen or heard of a fine mosaic, or a fresco executed or painted on the walls of a church to the memory of somebody in particular? If we adopted and employed mosaics or frescoes as memorials of the dead, as well as stained-glass windows, we would still be exercising a pious duty to our departed friends, and at the same time would be assisting to make the Temple of the Living God more comely and beautiful by adding some of the necessary colour finish to the walls of the church.

In a church at Birmingham there are a series of most beautiful windows in the chancel-end of the building, designed by Burne-Jones, that are magnificent in their glory of flaming crimson hues, and are superb examples of the artist's composition and design. One regrets, however, to find that the decoration of this church is typical of the usual embellishment of the modern House of Prayer, which generally begins and ends in the chancel windows.

Plate 3.—Design in Colour for the Decoration of Park Green Church, Macclesfield. By Author.

CHAPTER II
THE VALUE OF COLOUR AS APPLIED TO ARCHITECTURE

IT has been said that Architecture may be compared to a book, and that Sculpture and Painting are the illustrations which serve to explain the text and decorate the volume. It might be argued, however, that the text of the written book may be in itself a work of art, and therefore not require any explanatory illustrations or decorations. To a certain extent this may be quite true, but on the other hand a book will be more valuable, more useful, and more complete, as well as being more beautiful, by having the additional interest of a well-designed and appropriate setting of artistic and explanatory illustrations to embellish the text. And just as the written matter of the book should not be regarded as a mere background for the illustrations and decoration, neither should the architecture be so designed as to appear only as a background for the sculpture and painting, for the building is the important thing, but sculpture, painting, and ornamental decoration should be certainly employed to explain the architecture, to symbolise the use of the building, and to give additional interest and beauty to the fabric.

Colour in architecture ought to be employed in a structural sense, that is, it ought to be so used that it may help out, or confirm, the logical and indispensable features of a building that give to it the essential qualities of repose and stability, and the tones of colour, if judiciously selected and applied, will explain at a glance the various forms, features, divisions and sub-divisions of the architecture more rapidly and better than could possibly be hoped for in, say, a colourless or undecorated building. Therefore, in the diffused and somewhat darkened light of interiors the proper application of colour is of inestimable value, as an explanatory help in revealing the structural lines, the profiling of the mouldings, and the proportions of the architecture.

It is quite possible to decorate interiors in colour schemes of austere and extreme simplicity, in delicacy, in brilliancy, or in rich and full-toned splendour, in accordance with the nature and uses of the building, provided that we do not interfere with the essential quality of repose. In order that this important attribute of good architecture may be secured and maintained it is evident that neither sculptural nor coloured decoration should occur in isolated spots of interiors; they should not be dotted about, or applied here and there on walls, ceilings, pillars, mouldings, or other places, but should appear as essential and integral parts of the natural growth of a broad decorative scheme. It does not follow from this that certain parts of a building, such as the ceiling, the frieze, capitals of columns and the chancel-end or sanctuary of a church should not be more honoured by having a richer application of colour and ornament than the other parts of the building, but the inference is, that the latter should also be intelligently treated in colour and decoration, in a subordinate way, so that they will assist in the gradual leading up to the richer wealth of the more honoured and salient parts, and so become indispensable factors in promoting the unity of the entire scheme of decoration.

Coloured decoration which is only applied here and there in the interior of a building gives a spotty effect that is more than often futile and artificial. In the matter of church decoration it appears in our own country that just now it is more or less the custom to decorate the chancel-end of a church with a wealth of carving, stained glass, and richly-coloured ornamentation, and to leave the rest of the interior plain and colourless. We may be grateful, however, to find that the universal delight in colour, one of those things which we had "loved long since and lost awhile," is now revealing itself in modern days after centuries of absence, and is expressing itself, timidly, and in isolated spots, but perhaps as time goes on it will spread again slowly, and let us hope surely, from one end of the building to the other.

We must admit that a fine eye for colour is a natural gift as much as a fine perception for form and proportion, or as a fine ear for music, but a love for all these things may be inspired in us from the work and teachings of the great masters of former ages, and certainly a love for colour from the teachings of nature and the great schools of painting and decorative art. That there was a golden age of decorative painting in England in the fourteenth and fifteenth centuries we know from the remaining fragments of colour and decoration on the rood-screens and other parts of our old churches, and though the wall decorations have almost disappeared, the examples of painting which still remain on some of this old woodwork clearly testify to the importance of the English school of painting of the period mentioned.

We are more fortunate in our remaining possession of some of the finest stained glass in the world, which was designed and set up during the Middle Ages and early Renaissance times in England, and these rich and splendid "jewels set in silver setting" are a further proof of the keen delight of our early English decorators and craftsmen in the production of refined and beautiful colour.

[From a Water-colour by W. Davidson.

Plate 4.—Saint Michael: From a Painting on the Rood Screen, Ranworth Church, Norfolk. English, Early Sixteenth Century. From Water-colour by W. Davidson.

Many people ridicule the colouring of the Middle Ages as inharmonious and barbarous. Such absurd ideas in respect to the use of colour by the old decorators may have been derived from the knowledge that in early times the artist's palette was limited to three or four colours, besides black and white, and that these colours, such as red, blue, green and yellow, were applied, in decoration, in their full strength, as undoubtedly they generally were. But it ought to be remembered that, however crude the colours may be, it is their arrangement, quantity, and proportion as to surface area in the scheme of decoration, that makes, or mars, the harmony, and not their individual strength, purity or crudeness. The early decorators hardly ever used broken tones or half-tones in their colour arrangements, and perhaps this largely accounts for the mistaken views that some hold in regard to the decorative colouring of the Middle Ages. There is of course a great beauty in broken-toned colouring, which is in much favour in modern decoration, but it is not a matter of much difficulty to harmonise such broken tones and tints. A greater difficulty is to harmonise an arrangement of colours in their full strength of hue, a task for a great colourist; but this we know has often been done successfully in all the best periods of art, and it certainly was done by the old decorators of the Middle Ages in painting, mosaic, enamels, and stained glass, in spite of the limitation of their palette, or, shall we say, because of it?

In all the great periods of art there was certainly the keenest delight in colour. It is difficult for some of us to believe that the Parthenon and other Greek temples, and also all of our old cathedrals were at one time highly coloured, but they certainly were so shortly after they were built. The modern prejudice against the use of colour in architecture set in about the same time that sculpture also became, like painting, an independent art, which was about the beginning of the decadence of the Renaissance, at the end of the sixteenth century.

The architect, sculptor and painter should confer together, and if possible work in harmony with each other, so that when a cathedral, a church, a city hall, or any other public building is about to be erected, the complete scheme of the finished decoration should be formulated when the plans are being made. At any rate, the architect should always determine and keep in mind the style and nature of the subsequent colour effect and decoration, and so design his building in accordance with such preconceived ideas. That would be the ideal way to plan a building, after the uses of the structure were clearly defined, but unfortunately we are aware that the cases are few and rare in which the architect is enabled to do this, or that he lives long enough to see his ideas carried out. We might point out one notable instance of modern work where the architect's original ideas of the decoration are now being carried out, namely, in the new cathedral at Westminster. When planning this important building the architect thought out, very carefully, what the methods and nature of the colour finish were to be, and it is interesting and gratifying to find that the decoration of the brick shell of the building, including the main walls, the chapel, the crypt, and the sanctuary, are now being finished with a coloured marble sheathing, and with splendid mosaics, all of which he had made provision for in his original design.

CHAPTER III
THE DECORATIVE COLOURING OF INTERIORS

WHEN treating any building in colour, importance should be given obviously to the emphasising, and not to the effacement of the structural features, but when the building is deficient in such features, or very poor in this respect, it is the duty of the decorator to provide, in some measure, for this deficiency by dividing, for example, the large plain surfaces into panels, friezes, dadoes, spandrels, or other subdivisions, by the use of painted bands and lines, which may take the place of mouldings, but these painted bands and fillets should be treated flatly, and not in imitation of relief mouldings. These enclosing bands around panels, or large wall and ceiling subdivisions, may in certain cases be decorated with simple repeating patterns of ornament, and in others, if necessary, left in plain tints of colour. If, however, there should happen to be some permanent structural features, such as marble columns and entablatures, or woodwork in oak or mahogany, etc., already in the interior, and whose natural surfaces must be preserved, it follows then that the decorator must arrange his scheme of colour, not only to harmonise with the natural colour of these permanent structural features, but he must modify his colouring so that it will in no way overpower the colour of the permanent material, and so weaken the appearance of its structural character. On the other hand, great care should be taken to use only such tones in the colours as will prevent these permanent architectural features from having the undesirable effect of an extreme isolation in the building.

Whatever scale of colour is used in a building there should be a strict maintenance of its relationship between all the great divisions and subdivisions. The colourings of the latter may be treated as a sort of echo, in lower tones, of those of the former, but not so subdued as to give sharp contrasts. Every feature of the architecture, major or minor, should be well defined and balanced in colour harmony, so as to keep the general effect free from any startling abruptness or discordance, in order that they may all contribute to, and so preserve, the necessary breadth of treatment.

The principal or broad contrast in the colour scheme should be between the structural and non-structural parts, or the active parts such as columns, piers, ribs and cornices, and the inert surfaces, such as panels, ceilings, walls, vaults, and spandrels. The more intense and forcible expressions of colour relief ought to be used on selected portions of the structural forms, if they are not already of natural coloured materials, in order to unite them together, to give them a vigorous expression of life, and to emphasise their importance in the building.

Plate 5.—Design in Colour for the Decoration of the Town Hall,
Macclesfield. By Author.

TREATMENT OF WALLS.

There are no parts of a building that lend themselves to a more varied treatment in colour and decoration than the main walls of an interior, and this diversity

depends on the character, architectural style and uses of the building. It is obvious that the same treatment cannot well be given to the walls of a church, a theatre, a concert or an assembly room, and a private residence, though it often is done. Nor can an interior, like that of a public hall or palace, that may have such architectural features as columns, pilasters, and well-marked panellings, either of marble, stone, or of wood construction, be treated in a similar manner to that which may be proper for the walls of a room which may be devoid of any architectural features.

Then, again, we have to consider, before we set about the planning of the colour or decoration of a wall, whether it is to be partly covered with pictures in frames, or if great surfaces are to be coloured which will have nothing placed or hung upon them, or if the large surfaces are already divided into panels, or if the wall is to have a dado and a frieze, if there are already hangings or window curtains of a certain colour, and the carpet and furniture likewise. We may also have to decide whether our wall colouring is to be a harmony of analogy, or closely related colour tones, in accordance with the above objects in the room—that would be the simplest and safest method of colour treatment for the walls—or if it is to be a harmony of contrast in colour, which offers a more difficult problem, but if well done, would be more effective and interesting.

There are two other questions regarding the colour treatment of walls, or rather of interior colouring generally, which for the sake of argument we might consider, though they are of very little importance, and certainly have nothing like the importance which some decorators attach to them. We are told that before we begin the colouring of a room we are to ask ourselves "What is the aspect?" and also, "Is the room to be used mostly in the day, or mostly at night?" The questions seem logical enough, but we might well say in reply, that as regards the aspect of a room, what does it really matter whether the colouring is in a harmony of cool or warm, light or dark, arrangements of colour, provided we do obtain a harmony? Again, in our own countries, where we get so few days of long sunshine, is it really a matter of importance to decorate a room with a southern aspect in any way different from one with a northern aspect? The greatest decorators of the finest periods never seemed to trouble themselves much about aspects. They were more interested in producing good decoration, and in the planning of fine colour schemes. As regards the decoration and colouring of a room for day, or for night uses, we may say at once, that if we except the interiors of theatres, there are hardly any rooms, in either public or private buildings and residences, that are not used both in the day and at night, so we may safely disregard the problem of colouring that is to be viewed by artificial light, for in nine cases out of ten, at least, ordinary interiors are seen, and ordinary rooms used, both in the day and night. It is best, therefore, to arrange our colour schemes so that they will look harmonious in the daylight, and such colouring will not suffer much by artificial light, provided the room is well lighted by electric or incandescent gas lamps, and is not in a state of low illumination, or semi-darkness.

We shall say something later on in reference to the changes which some colours undergo when seen in artificial light. (Plate 13.)

Plate 6.—Colour Arrangement for the Decoration of a Room.

We offer a few suggestions for the general colouring of walls in rooms of an ordinary residence or in public buildings, namely:—If a red is decided upon it should be of a deep pink slightly broken or toned with a very little blue and yellow; if the colour is to be of a yellowish tone, it ought to be pale and golden inclining to a light brown; if blue it should be of a pale greenish blue, or of any tint between that and a greyish ultramarine; a deep blue tone should never be used for large wall spaces. If greens are to be used in large spaces they should be, if pale, more pure in colour than in the case of deep greens; the latter tones should be less pure and more grey, in order to avoid rankness of hue.

Plate 7.—Three Suggestions of Colour Tints for Painted Walls or Paperhangings, as Backgrounds for Framed Pictures.

These suggestions apply to the colours of either painted walls, or to the tints of paperhangings, if the latter be used as wall-coverings. Large expanses of wall surfaces when painted in a single tint have usually a dry and uninteresting appearance; to avoid this, and at the same time to give the wall the effect of being treated in a single tone of colour, the surface, after being painted in the chosen colour, should have another thin application of a tint, slightly lighter, or darker than the previous coating, stippled over the latter, or the thin, and different, shade of colour may be applied with the brush, and immediately after the application it should be partially wiped off with clean rags. This operation will give the wall surface a slightly mottled and lively appearance, and will remove the dead and monotonous uniformity usually seen on painted walls when the work is finished in the more solid and flat methods of execution. (See Plate 7.)

We give as suggestions of colours the three examples on Plate 7, which we think suitable as background tints for the walls of rooms on which pictures would be hung. Any of these colours might be used on the walls of a picture gallery or in rooms that contained pictures in gold or in black frames, either for the colour tints of paint, if used, or for the tints of paperhangings, but for choice we think the brownish tinted—middle illustration—would be on the whole the most satisfactory of the three. If the walls are to be painted they should be finished in a stippled manner, as described above, but if a paperhanging is used the stippled effect would be obtained by a very small self-coloured, lighter or darker pattern, or by some other method of superimposed lines or dots on the red, brown, or grey-green ground.

TREATMENT OF CEILINGS: VAULTED OR FLAT.

When decorating curved surfaces, such as vaulted ceilings, domes, or the semi-dome of an apse, when they are not sectionally divided by mouldings, or archivolts, it is extremely difficult to preserve the proper appearance of their sections or surfaces, especially when they are treated pictorially, or with a diaper, or all-over-pattern of ornament. In such cases it is necessary, as the custom was with the majority of the old mosaic artists and fresco painters, to subdivide these vaulted or domed ceilings into proportionate parts, running either in a vertical or in a horizontal direction, by bands, or lines, thus supplying the needed substitute for mouldings or relief divisional lines. Even if these bands and lines were left out, and the decoration designed in a series of horizontal, vertical, or arched divisions, forming rows of figures or ornament, an appearance of constructive stability would be given to the scheme of decoration and so prevent any confusion as to the true section of the vaulted surface.

When a ceiling of a large hall or of a church is to be decorated, whether the surface be flat or curved, it is generally necessary to interpose a band of colour, either plain, or with a pattern on it, between the cornice, ribs, or archivolts and the field or panel, so that the structural abruptness between these features may be modified and softened, and that an artistical alliance may be created between the colouring of the panel and that of the cornice under the flat ceiling, or between the ribs and the vaulted surface, respectively.

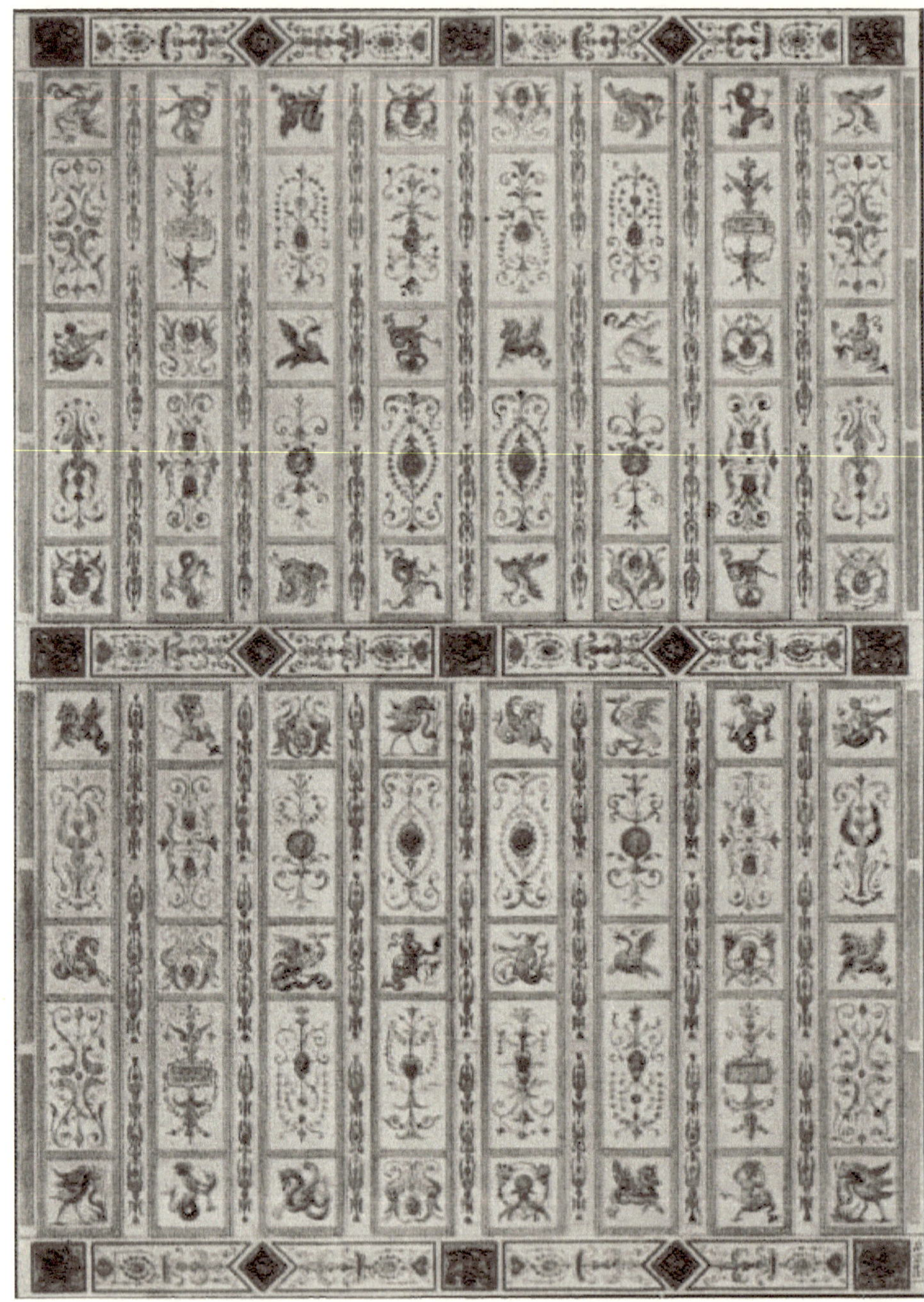

Plate 8.—Design in Colour for the Decoration of a Morning Room Ceiling at Queen's Gate, London. By Author.

The ceilings of interiors, whether flat or vaulted, provide admirable fields for colour and decoration. The greatest attention was given to them by the artists of the Italian Renaissance. Even when the rest of the interiors were simple or almost plain, in regard to decorative treatment, the ceiling was hardly ever neglected. (Plate 21.) Some of the finest Italian art is found on the ceilings of the churches and palaces. For example, Michel Angelo's masterpiece in painting was the ceiling of the Sistine Chapel; there are also Raffaelle's ceiling decorations in the Stanze of the Vatican; Pinturrichio's richly-coloured ceilings in the Borgia Apartments, and those of his in the "Sala Piccolomini" at Siena, in the choir of Santa Maria del Popolo, Rome, in Santa Maria Maggiore at Spello, and in the Chapel of the Sala di Cambio at Perugia, where he worked with Perugino. Many important ceiling decorations were painted by Raffaelle's pupils, Giulio Romano, Perino del Vaga and Giovanni da Udine, in the palaces at Mantua, the Villa Madama, some in Venice and Genoa, others in the Vatican and in the Castel Angelo, at Rome, etc. There is also the ceiling of elaborate panelling, in which figure subjects alternate with arabesques in the Chapel of the Palazzo Vecchio at Florence, painted by Ridolfo Ghirlandaio. Ceilings of a later date, heavy in their mouldings and ornamentation, exist in the churches and palaces of Venice, and other places, which were painted with pictorial subjects by Paul Veronese and Tintoretto. The list of Italian painted ceilings would be almost endless, and we have only mentioned a few to point out the importance attached to ceiling decoration in Italy. The Italian ceilings were usually moulded, and were divided into a series of panels, lozenged-shaped, square, oblong, and circular, and where the relief mouldings did not exist, the decorator supplied their place by bands and enclosing lines, or even in some cases by feigned mouldings in colour, and sometimes by low relief stucco. Most of the ceilings were coloured in the brightest possible tints, and gold was also freely used, not only for heightening the salient parts of mouldings and carved enrichments, but often as backgrounds to the pictorial work and ornamental patterns. The gold backgrounds were in most cases slightly toned with a glaze of warm transparent brown, or were treated with a fine mesh-like pattern of crossed lines, to enrich and also to modify the raw brilliancy of the gold. Another effective way of using gold was the common employment of gold stars and spots over bright red or blue backgrounds. This was usually done in cases where gold was used in the bands, or in ornament on the bands, which surrounded the panels having the bright-coloured backgrounds.

If one may be permitted to criticise the splendid Italian painted ceilings, it might be pointed out that, generally speaking, the rich and deep colouring was in many cases too dark, which often produced a lowering effect in this architectural feature of the room, especially in cases where the ceiling was only of a moderate height. It is only very lofty ceilings that can safely be treated in strong and moderately dark colours, and in proportion to the lowness of a ceiling the colouring should tend to become lighter in scale. The greatest weight or strength of colour on a flat ceiling should be kept in the corners, and near the cornice. This will help to give a more raised appearance to the centre, or at least it will determine, in an effective manner, the more perfect flatness of the surface, as all flat ceilings have a tendency to appear lower in the centre than at the sides. The general colour scheme of a ceiling should be arranged with due regard to even distribution, not only of the colour values, but of the tints and hues, and if gold is used great care must be taken that it is also evenly distributed, so as to prevent any spottiness that would be due to the inequality of its application; in short a perfect balance of the colours and gold must be maintained respectively, although it may not be necessary to have a mechanical symmetry either in the colouring, ornamental patterns, or in the infilling of the panels, or other subdivisions.

MOULDINGS.

One of the most distinguishing characteristics of the architectural styles are the mouldings, so much so, that a building having no mouldings is almost, if not entirely, devoid of architectural expression; it may be classed as a structure, but hardly as true architecture, for the style, and even the date of a building may be often determined by the design of its mouldings alone. Ruskin has said, "Never give mouldings separate colours," but he adds that "he knows this is heresy." He is right if he means that the individual members of a group of mouldings should not be "picked out" in too decided or separate colours. What should be avoided is the possible danger of detaching them too much from each other. Contrasting colours should be used sparingly, and only to distinguish the larger and more structural members from those of the smaller ones. Simple explanation of their contours only is wanted, and not any appearance of detachment. As a rule, the more numerous and elaborate the group of mouldings the less contrast in their colour treatment is required. But, on the other hand, if a well-balanced colour harmony is obtained by treating a group of mouldings in separate colours, provided there is no appearance of detachment, and that the effect of harmonious unity of colour as a leading motive is secured, then we should say that this particular treatment would be justified. There are many instances where groups of mouldings have been treated in strong contrasting colours, in work of the fifteenth and sixteenth centuries, which are examples of successful colouring.

THE CORNICE.

The cornice in an ordinary room should be treated in colour as part of the wall, and not as belonging to the ceiling, for the cornice is the crown of the wall, and is not part of the ceiling. The value of a cornice in a room, as an architectural feature, is to soften the harsh divisional line between the ceiling and the wall, but this effect is destroyed if the cornice is left white or coloured like the ceiling, and not treated in colour to show that it belongs to the wall. As a general rule, the deep and recessed hollows in the cornice should be coloured fairly strong, as weak tints are lost or become grey when they are in shadow, but large spaces, such as coved hollows, that happen to be well lighted, should not be treated so strongly in colour. Prominent edges and fillets of the cornice mouldings should be either light in colour or gilt.

[From a Drawing by W. Davidson.

Plate 9.—Decorated Mouldings: From the Rood Screen, Ranworth Church, Norfolk. English, Early Sixteenth Century. Drawn by W. Davidson.

The Frieze.

The frieze of a public hall, assembly-room, or of a room in an ordinary house, is an architectural feature which always forms a fine field for colour and decoration, in sculpture or in painting. In the earliest, and in all great periods of art, the frieze was that part of the building which received the richest treatment. The best art of the ancient Mesopotamian nations was lavished on the coloured enamelled friezes, and the chief glory of the Parthenon was its sculptured frieze. The treatment, where pictorial or ornamental, admits of more elaboration in design and a richer application of colour than any other part of the room. (Plate 10.) If an interior has an important frieze decoration, it is not so necessary to have much colour or decoration on the ceiling. When tinting the cornice mouldings over the frieze it is extremely important that the dominant colours in the frieze should be "echoed" in some of the members of the cornice.

A frieze is of more architectural value in a room than a dado, for it is sufficient of itself to give an architectural aspect to a room; but if there is a dado it would obviously be coloured somewhat darker than the walls, whether it was in wood, or only as a painted feature, and its moulding or "chair rail" would be coloured so as to harmonise with the dado, because it is also the crown or cornice of that feature.

As regards the debatable question of the imitation of relief mouldings and other architectural features on painted walls and ceilings, there are many precedents for doing so, some of which we will speak of further on, but this can only be successfully done when the decorator has a good knowledge of architecture and knows exactly what to do, like Michel Angelo when he divided the plain surface of the ceiling of the Sistine Chapel into panels and niches by means of imitative structural forms and mouldings, in order to separate and enclose his magnificent painted series of scriptural subjects, prophets and sibyls. The imitation of architectural features in painted light and shade may not be logical, but when a great artist does such things, we are obliged to accept them without much criticism, as we accept the work of a great poet who makes his own grammar.

Treatment of Woodwork.

The question of whether to paint in colour the woodwork such as doors, window-frames and wainscoting of interiors, or to leave them in the natural colour of the wood, depends chiefly on the kind of wood employed in their construction. It would be wrong, for example, to advise the painting or colouring of the more valuable kinds of wood such as oak, mahogany, walnut, ebony, or any rare kind of wood, in any way other than that which would deepen or make richer the natural tone of the material by the application of a varnish, and of such a varnish as would only intensify the natural beauty of the wood, but not produce anything like a polished surface. It would be better to accept the natural colour of such woods, and to scheme the colouring of walls and ceiling to harmonise with the colour of the woodwork in such cases, especially if in addition to the door and window-framing there happened to be a considerable amount of wainscoting or wood panelling in the room.

Plate 10.—Design in Colour for a Frieze Decoration. By Author.

In the medieval and earlier periods, however, whether in churches, palaces, or in smaller houses, even the more valuable woods, especially oak, were always painted and decorated in colours. The natural colour, or the rarity of valuable woods, did not as a rule prevent them from being treated in colour like the other parts of the buildings. Romanesque and Gothic wooden ceilings and rood-screens, though constructed of oak or other hard woods, were invariably treated in colour and partly gilt.

The simplest and perhaps the more satisfactory way of treating the woodwork of an ordinary room in colour would be in selected tones of the colour which appears on the larger wall spaces, but whatever the hue that may be used on the woodwork it should be of two or three shades of the selected colour, forming a harmony of closely related tones. (See Plates 6 and 11.) The woodwork may be in some cases of a different scheme of colouring from the walls, as in such instances where there is a dado of wood or a wainscot of wood panelling, but where the doors or windows appear as isolated features in large wall spaces, the most satisfactory way of treating them in colour is to paint them in analogous tones of the wall colour. If gold occurs in the frieze or on the cornice mouldings, the fillets, or smaller members of the door frames and panel mouldings should also be gilt.

Plate 11.—Colour Arrangements for Doors and Woodwork.

CHAPTER IV
THE COLOURING OF EXTERIORS

THE colouring of the exteriors of important buildings should be, if possible, effected by the use of the constructive materials, such as stone, marble, granite and coloured terra-cotta in conjunction with panels and friezes, etc., of enamelled tiles or mosaic, and even in the case of less pretentious buildings a good deal might be done by ordinary painting. Stucco plastered exteriors, however, should not necessarily be painted in a uniform stone colour. Stone and soft bricks get black in cities, but hard bricks retain their colour much better. A highly polished material, such as granite or marble, does not go well with freestone, owing to the violent contrast between the polished and dull surfaces; also, any highly polished surface reflects light in such a way that to the sight the form is often altered. Granite polished with emery brings out the natural colour without giving a glaze to it, and is therefore better for an outdoor effect. Bronze sheathing on doors and bronze window and door framing, when it is not too dark in tone, goes well with a grey granite building, and when such a building has some panels of mosaic, or of coloured marble, such as "opus Sectile," the colour scheme is very effective. These materials are now being used very much in some important buildings in the continental cities.

In using coloured marbles, the best effects, as a rule, are obtained when two kinds only are used together, or merely one colour with white, such as black and white, red and white, green and white or purple and white. The finest early Italian marble altars, pulpits, and monuments generally conform to one of these simple colour arrangements. The principal parts of these works are executed in white marble and have only one coloured marble introduced for columns, pilasters, friezes, and panels at the bases and pediments. It may be mentioned that the white marble of these monuments is yellowish in tone, and the black somewhat greenish, thus producing a soft and mellow effect. At Palermo and Naples there is a great deal of marble work of the later Renaissance and modern times which has inlaid floral arabesques in various coloured marbles, such as black, brown, orange and red, all in combination, the greater part of which is unsatisfactory as it lacks repose, owing to the harshness of the contrasting colours.

A notable exception to the use of two, or at most three, kinds of marble in combination is seen in the magnificent "opus Alexandrinum" floor pavements, and in other marble work of the Byzantine buildings, where three kinds have been used, namely, porphyry, serpentine and white, with sometimes little portions of yellow, but the purple of the porphyry and the green of the serpentine, with their variegated tints, are colours which are in complete accordance with each other, and the effect of this arrangement is always pleasant and harmonious.

There is every reason why public buildings should be erected in natural or artificially coloured materials. Such coloured materials would not be more expensive than the grey, drab, and white stone and marble which is now used so much for exterior elevations. If we cannot have rich colouring on the outsides of our public buildings, we might at least be permitted to have schemes of colour that would present quiet and restrained harmonies, so that, even in a modest degree, they would contribute to our pleasure by counteracting some of the greyness and gloom that overshadows and often conceals the architectural beauty of many buildings in our large towns and cities.

Architects and sculptors, as a rule, are responsible for the appearance of the exteriors of buildings, and they only in exceptional cases appear to have a love for colour, but they should remember that colour appeals, if not to everybody, to a considerably large section of the public, which includes both cultured and uncultured people, who can appreciate a coloured building, but are not much interested in seeing a colourless exterior.

Some of the simplest and inexpensive examples of exterior structural colouring may be obtained by the use of red brick, and common stone dressings on the façade of a building, if to this could be added some notes of grey-blue in terra-cotta, or tiles, in bands, borders, or in panels. Mosaic in panels would be better still, but we leave that out on the score of expense. Such an example as this colour arrangement may be seen in many buildings in Florence, Milan, and in the northern towns of Italy. We might mention one, that of the front of the Hospital of the Innocents, in Florence, which is a yellow-red brick elevation with severe columns and arches of a warm-coloured stone, and in the spandrels between the arches are the grey-blue and white roundels of Delia Robbia glazed earthenware, the whole effect being a pleasant and warm colour arrangement, and besides being extremely simple, it is certainly very effective, and an admirable example of structural colouring.

At Verona, Venice, and many other places in Italy there are fine examples of this style of exterior colouring where the red bricks give the dominant tone, whether terra-cotta or stone be used for the dressings, or glazed earthenware heraldic panels, mosaic, or fresco are added to give the balance of blue, or other sharper notes of pure colour, that may be required to complete the harmony.

It is a matter well known that in Northern Germany, Belgium, Holland, and in England red brick buildings with stone and terra-cotta dressings and sculptured work were erected as manor houses, palaces, and every kind of public building, in the fifteenth and sixteenth centuries, most of which were fine examples, not only of architecture, but of exterior colouring.

The front of the Doge's Palace at Venice is an example of suitable application of colour to public buildings. The sculpture and mouldings are in white marble, and the wall surface has a chequered pattern of marble slabs of a pale rose colour and white Istrian stone.

Fresco paintings and mosaic have often been employed in Italy on the exteriors of churches and palaces. There is a beautiful bit of heraldic painting, alternating with cardinals' hats placed in squares, on a wall behind the Duomo of Verona. This, however, and nearly all exterior wall paintings have suffered very much by the weather in course of time, and such decoration has no chance of lasting compared with the colour of the more permanent materials of stone, marble, tiles, or mosaic.

In Germany, much more than other countries, exterior colour-painting and decoration has always found great favour. Even to-day the exteriors of many buildings, especially hostelries and restaurants, are painted as they were in the sixteenth century. A great revival of colour decoration took place in Germany, as it did also in France, about the middle of the last century. We shall consider this at more length when making an historical survey of the subject in later chapters, and endeavour to describe some of the methods and principles of colour decoration adopted and carried out by the old decorators of England and the continental nations. Before leaving, however, this portion of our subject it may be useful and interesting to notice an important example of Venetian exterior polychromy of the late medieval period.

The building in question is known as the Ca' D'Oro, or "Golden House," so called on account of the great quantity of gilding that it formerly had on its façade. This building must have been erected on the site of a former medieval palace, for the rebuilding of it was begun in 1424, contemporary with that of the Piazzeta façade of the Ducal Palace at Venice. The architect or "stone-mason" was Giovanni Buon, who was assisted by his son, Bartolomeo, the palace being erected for a nobleman named Marino Contarini, at St. Sophia on the Grand Canal. The existing documents, which consist of the original memoranda of Contarini, dated 1431-2, and preserved among the papers of the Procurators of St. Mark's, give in detail the orders for the gold and colours, and how they were to be used in the decoration of the façade. From these and also from the traces of the colour and gold which Signor G. Boni found on parts of the building in 1885, we are enabled to form an estimate of the polychromatic decorations of this medieval palace, which may serve as an illustration of the external colour-decoration of the period.

From these evidences we find that the balls of Istrian stone which decorated the embattlements were gilt, also the carved mouldings, the abacus of each capital, lions, shields, dentels, rose-flowers, and other salient points of the carvings. The backgrounds of capitals, soffits, some shields and bands were painted ultramarine blue, "fine azure ultramarine, in such a manner that it may last longer" (that is, twice coated). The blue ground of the soffits was studded with small golden stars. It is interesting to note how all the stonework was painted in the early times, when it is mentioned that all the red stones of the façade and the red dentels were to be painted with oil and varnish in still deeper tones of red, "so that they will look red." It appears that this was done in order to give a look of uniformity to the red Verona *Broccatello* marble, which, being composed of the detritus of ammonites, had a variegated, or patchy-like appearance when newly cut, and therefore its effect, when new, did not find favour in the eyes of the decorator, as perhaps he thought that in its virgin state its appearance disturbed the broad colour effect he was aiming for. The crowning cornice was painted with white lead and oil, and also in a like manner the roses and vines on the façade. The backgrounds of the latter carved decoration, and that of the fields of the cusps of the window tracery and of the cornice foliage were painted black, in order to give the effect of penetration.

The parts of the façade which were painted white were those of bluish or yellowish Istrian stone, the natural colour of which the Venetians did not like, so they generally obliterated it with a coating of white paint. In the memoranda it is also stated that the stone battlements were to be "painted and veined, to make them look like marble."

The imitation of marbles and woods by painting the commoner stone, or inferior wood in simulation of the more costly materials, though rightly condemned as a common practice by purists has, however, been largely practised by the decorators of primitive Greece, Pompeii, Rome, and of the East, as well as of the Renaissance and later periods. The old decorators had no scruples in regard to the painting of plaster or common stone to make it look like marble; but generally in such examples the imitation was more strictly confined to objects and surfaces where the more costly materials would have been used if sufficient means had been available to procure them.

The modern practice of imitating a costly wood by graining an inferior one hardly ever obtained in the earlier periods; the old decorators often enough painted all kinds of wood in any arbitrary way or colour, but they did not grain them to simulate other woods. Although the imitation of wood by graining is not practised so much to-day as it was in the Victorian time, there is still a good deal of it done. Even worse than this is the modern practice of erecting wooden columns and entablatures as shop fronts, especially those of public-houses and gin-palaces, in simulation of a stone construction, which may be an excusable sham, but there is no reason why this stone construction in wood should be painted to imitate costly marble, which only makes a double sham. We can call to mind the instance of some large and heavy doors in a Government building of this country, which are, of course, made in panelled wood, but have been painted to imitate grey granite! The reader can think that the limit of imitative painting is here reached, if he can imagine the deception that is presented of two slabs of heavy granite swinging on hinges.

In the case of the Ca' D'Oro battlements, and of similar imitations of marble in the painted decoration of late medieval buildings in Venice, we can see the expression of a striving after the rich effects of colour that were obtained in the earlier Byzantine architecture by the use of the real marbles, which were employed to give the structural and permanent colour to edifices built in that style. It ought to be remembered that the Venetian Gothic architecture, more especially in colouring—and we might safely say all Venetian art of later periods with its rich and beautiful colour—was strongly influenced by the splendour of Byzantine and Eastern colouring, as expressed in the mosaics, enamels, and richly-coloured marbles that were used so much to line the walls inside and outside of the Byzantine churches and palaces.

Although such coloured decoration as that of the façade of the Ca' D'Oro might be classed as a decadent and artificial system, in so far as it was an imitation, or an attempt in applied colour at the survival of the more permanent Byzantine coloured architecture, still the general effect of the colour scheme, where full-toned blues, reds, black, white, and gold were frankly employed, must have been extremely rich and interesting, when seen in the radiant sunshine, and reflected in the waters of the Grand Canal. We might add that the colouring of this medieval palace, in common with that employed on all Venetian buildings of that time, was also in a great measure a reflex of the powerful and sensuous colouring of the East, which strongly influenced, if it was not indeed the chief source of the distinctive colour harmony that was the crown and glory of Venetian art.

CHAPTER V

ON THE USE AND MODIFICATION OF COLOUR IN DECORATION

JUST as the aims of the painter of pictures are quite divergent from those of the decorator, so is the use of colour in the representation of natural objects and of natural phenomena divergent from that of the latter's in his employment of tints in coloured decoration. The painter of pictures is at liberty to use unlimited tints and shades of one colour, or of any number of colours, to represent the facts or effects of nature in realistic or in imaginative art, that is to say, he can make the greatest possible use of gradation both in colour and in light and shade, but the decorator is limited in the matter of colour gradation, and still more limited in the matter of light and shade, to the use of a few tints of closely related tones, and, as a rule, he must use them in a series of flat tints, with little or no light and shade, and which may or may not be separated from each other by contours or outlines of neutral or different colours.

The aim of the decorator is to beautify surfaces by the use of colour, so he selects or creates his tints and shades, which may be of extremely rich and deeply saturated hues, heightened perhaps with the addition of silver or gold, or he may use schemes of sober tints of broken colours; but the aim of the picture painter is to respect the colouring of nature and to produce another kind of beauty, which if not always strictly imitative of natural forms and facts in colour and drawing, must at least show that its foundations are laid on the solid ground of nature. Colour is therefore used by the artist-painter in a limited sense, in so far as it is imitative of any particular scene or natural effect which he may desire to record, but the choice of the decorator is unlimited, for he can always invent his own colour schemes. And as the latter is justified in disregarding shadows and gradation in the rendering of his decorative forms, even when they are derived from nature, he is equally free to use any colour in an arbitrary way on such forms instead of their natural or local colour, provided that it does not interfere with the harmony and balance of his colour scheme. The old Gothic glass painters, for example, who produced some of the finest coloured glass, did not hesitate to colour the feet or the hands of their figures a vivid green, a crimson, or a brilliant blue, though the other flesh portions of the same figure would be in the natural colour, if they found it necessary to have any of those colours in such parts of the design where the feet or hands happened to be. Although we should not agree with this arbitrary colour treatment of natural forms, it only emphasises the fact that the old designers looked upon their figure compositions as simply units or integral parts of the general colour scheme, and nothing more or less than legitimate decoration.

The decorator may design his ornamental forms on the bases of natural ones, and may, by colouring them in tints suggested by nature, produce a beautiful decorative work, which indeed has often been done. Still, he is free to frankly disregard the natural or local colour of such forms if the latter does not suit his purpose, and may use any other colours that will enable him to produce the best effect and most satisfactory decoration. In any case there should be no attempt to imitate either the colouring or forms of nature in a realistic sense, however much he may make use of suggestions from natural forms and objects. If purely natural forms, such as those of birds, animals, or the human figure are introduced into decoration, they should be firmly outlined in some neutral colour in order to show that they are only intended as portions of the decorative scheme and not in the sense of realistic representations. Accurate representations of natural forms and photographic realism should be avoided in decoration. If the Byzantine mosaicists had drawn, or could have drawn, their figures better, they might have produced worse decoration, and might have failed to express the essentials of decorative art.

The greater part of modern polychrome decoration, not only on buildings but on nearly every description of handmade objects or manufactured goods that have pretensions to artistic claims, is only misapplied painting which has usurped the place of true decoration. This kind of semi-pictorial work came into vogue about the beginning of the seventeenth century in Italy and France, and gradually spread and developed in other European countries, so to-day there is still a great demand for this kind of art which is neither genuine decoration nor painting. Interior surfaces of buildings, textile hangings, carpets, all kinds of pottery, and almost every kind of object that presents a surface for decoration is treated with naturalistic transcripts of flowers, birds, animals, the human figure, as well as copies of landscapes and architectural views, all represented in a pictorial manner with more or less merit, but all misapplied work. Such meretricious merchandise is welcomed and purchased by a very large section of the public, who are unable to distinguish between true and false decoration.

Decoration in Monochrome.—The simplest form of coloured decoration is monochromatic, that is, where one colour is used or where several tints of any one colour are used. This kind of colour treatment is often very satisfactory for the walls, ceilings, and woodwork of any ordinary room, where the pictures on the walls, the carpet, hangings, furniture and ornamental objects all combine to furnish the sharper and more contrasting colour notes that may be required. In such monochromatic decoration lighter and darker shades of the selected colour are used, the lighter and less intense tints being spread over the larger spaces, while the more intense and purer shades would be on the mouldings and on the smaller subdivisions of the architecture. The choice of the particular colour selected for any monochromatic scheme will in a measure depend on the uses of the room as well as on the decorative taste and feeling for colour. Monochromatic colouring may be enlivened by the use of gold in narrow lines or in small quantities, such as in the gilding of the fillets of door mouldings and cornices, etc.

Use of gold in decoration.—Gold should not be used in large quantities in any scheme of decoration, except in backgrounds where it would be partially covered with ornamentation, or else it will be liable to lose its precious quality, and so look vulgar and common. Where gold is used in great quantities, such as we see in the gaudy gold and white decoration of some state assembly-rooms, it completely loses its quality of preciousness, and in proportion to the increase of the quantity used, it becomes cheap-looking and appears more like brass than gold. If gold must be used lavishly in the decoration of state rooms it ought to be toned down with some transparent brown colour which would tend to make it still richer, and would destroy the tinselly or brassy appearance which large masses of gilding always present to the eye. Where gold was used in backgrounds of figure or ornamental compositions by the Italian artists, its natural glare was usually toned down either by having a net-work of lines, or a fine tracery pattern, or sometimes a fine diaper or checker pattern painted on it in black or dark brown. Also the surface, previous to the gilding of it, was sometimes prepared with a rough texture, in order to prevent it from having the objectionable shine that is common to the gilding of smooth surfaces, and to enable the spectator to see the real colour of the precious metal. Gold grounds look better when the surface is slightly curved, for all gilded flat surfaces, unless modified by one of the methods we have mentioned above, will either appear glaringly bright or very dark according to the position from which they are seen. It may also be mentioned that gold has in common with white, or very pale colours, the effect of spreading, so that thin lines, or delicate tracery patterns in gold, on a dark, or moderately dark coloured ground, always appear to look broader than they really are, this being due to the spreading effect of light which is reflected to the eye by the brilliancy of gold, or white.

Coloured decoration on gold grounds ought to be outlined in black, or some very dark colour, in order to prevent the gold from overpowering the colour and making it look ineffective. When highly relieved enrichments are gilt, the ground behind them may be "picked out" in strong colour, such as vermilion, deep cobalt blue, or black in cases where an effect of penetration is desired, but in proportion to the lowness of the relief the background colouring may be lessened in strength or intensity. It must be pointed out, however, that ornament in very low relief, if gilded, will require a more strongly coloured background than in the case of ornament that may be simply coloured, but not gilt.

The small interval, or concord of closely related tones.—It might be suggested that the natural development, or sequence of purely monochromatic colouring to a full and rich polychromy would be of that kind of colour harmony which is known as *the small interval*, which, in decoration, is expressed by the concord of closely related colour tones. It may be also defined as a harmony of colour analogy, a kind of gradation where colours and their tints are separated by a little distance or interval from each other in the chromatic circle. The colouring of natural objects and phenomena afford endless examples of the small interval. The plumage of birds, wings of insects, foliage of trees and plants, flowers, shells, some minerals, and the sunset sky may be mentioned as some of the illustrations of this kind of harmonious colour gradation, where the various tints and shades of closely related colours are cunningly arranged by nature in delicate, yet decided contrasts, not of hue, but of analogous tones. For example, a green-blue may pass into a violet-blue, by a gradual series of separated tints, but the latter colour must be kept at the shade of violet just before it is overcome by red, and the former must not be overpowered by yellow. The colour of a peacock's neck-plumage affords a good illustration of this kind of green-blue to violet-blue colouring by gradation of shades. A similar gradation is where an orange-red passes gradually into a crimson-red, but neither yellow in the first-named colour nor blue in the crimson must be permitted to overcome them. The decorator being concerned with the use of broken colours—that is, pure colours modified by mixture of black, white or grey—for the covering of large spaces such as walls, ceilings and woodwork panels, can therefore adopt the principle of the small interval in architectural colouring with advantage and success, by using any group of closely related colours for his scheme; and further, if he desires to intensify or enliven the latter, he can do so by the use of small quantities of other contrasting colours introduced in the cornice, frieze or mouldings, or in lines, bands and other forms of painted ornamentation, and, if necessary, the whole of the decoration might be heightened by gilding.

Coloured decoration on coloured grounds.—The use of coloured grounds, and especially those of contrasting colours, postulates the more complex forms of polychromatic decoration, where a good number of widely separated tints and shades of various colours are employed in any one scheme.

In polychromatic schemes of colouring there are certain laws which must be respected, regarding the relation of one colour to another, their modification of tint or shade, as affected by their position, and the strength or weakness of the light which illuminates them, however much may be left to the good taste and feeling for colour which the decorator may possess. All these essentials have to be considered, for it is not so much a question of rich and glowing colour schemes, or sober, quiet and subdued arrangements, but to obtain a harmonious colour finish in either. The decorator must aim for, and if possible obtain, a proper balance of colour, not so much for the achievement of uniformity, as for that of unity and repose. In order to obtain unity he must therefore see that even in the most complex polychromy a perfect balance of the colours is the first consideration, and of the utmost importance. In decoration we have both colour and form, but colour in decorative art is the more important of the two. A certain balance is looked for in ornamental or pictorial fillings of panels, for example, or even in the secondary ornamentation of painted bands, stiles, and other minor surfaces, but the repetition of exactly similar forms on such surfaces is by no means essential, but on the contrary produces monotony. In the matter of colour the case is reversed, for it is very important that there should be a decided repetition of colour, even to the point of symmetry, in architectural colouring, if the balance is to be maintained. There must be "echoes" or "recalls" of the same, or very similar, tints and shades in ceilings, walls, woodwork, and other parts of interior colouring if the qualities of good decoration, such as breadth, repose, and rhythm are to be secured. The rhythm of colour in decoration is of far more importance than that of the ornamental forms.

**Plate 12.—Mosaic Panel: From the Cartoon of the Mosaic in St. Paul's
Cathedral, London: Melchizedek Blessing Abraham.
By Sir W. B. Richmond, K.C.B., R.A.**

These laws and principles apply to all kinds of architectural decoration and
their colour schemes, but if possible with more force to the richer and more complex polychromy, where pure and intense colours are employed with others of
lesser intensity, together with gold, silver, white and black.

Contours, or outlines.—Coloured ornament or pictorial decoration on coloured
grounds ought to be outlined, especially so if the ornament or decoration does not
differ much in colour from that of the ground. Even colours that greatly contrast
with each other ought to be outlined to prevent them from having the appearance

of mixing with each other, for most colours will not show their true value unless they are outlined with a neutral one such as black, white or gold, or with some lighter or darker colour than their own. The general rule is, that if the superimposed ornament is of a lighter colour than the ground, provided that it is not excessively light, it should be outlined with a still lighter colour, but if darker than the ground, the outline should be still darker.

Certain ornamental compositions, such as arabesques that are painted in light and shade on a coloured or gold ground, may not require decided contours. The absence of outlines on such ornament is not so detrimental to them as it would be to decoration that is painted in flat tints, because such arabesques or tracery are sufficiently relieved by their light and shade treatment, and are usually painted in dark and intense colours, if the background is white or light in tint, and on dark-coloured grounds they are generally executed in lighter and brighter colours on the dark ground.

Light or pale-coloured grounds are made to appear deeper in hue by painting a fine tracery of a similar but deeper and purer colour on them, or by "powdering" small patterns or spots of such colour on these light surfaces, and a deeply-coloured ground may have its colour considerably lightened by superimposing on it a fine tracery pattern in white. Also, a fine pattern painted in two distinct colours, or a series of small dots in two colours, evenly distributed on a brightly-coloured ground, will change the colour scheme by causing another, and a new colour to appear, when the work is viewed from a distance. All these changes and effects are produced in an optical sense, for the new colours are those which are due to the mixtures of the painted ones on the retina of the eye, as they are not the inherent colours of the decoration. Though these optical colours are not, as a rule, purposely sought for, yet a consideration of them is valuable to the decorator. Much of the beauty of certain kinds of decoration is due to them; for example, that of the strongly coloured Moorish schemes, where red and gold, which supplies the yellow, combine to produce an optical orange colour, and where blue and gold mingle to produce a violet, when seen at some distance away. In the same way when white is introduced into these colour arrangements, as in the outlining of the patterns, or in numerous small touches, paler tints of the new colours are optically produced. Other illustrations of new colours that are produced in an optical sense may be noticed in the old glass of the Romanesque and early Gothic periods, where the magnificent purple and violet hues are more than often obtained by the juxtaposition of deeply saturated reds and crimsons with intense and rich blues, that notwithstanding their separation by the leading of the stained glass, which acts as black outlines, mingle together and produce rich purples and violets when seen at a distance. It has been noticed that even the negative shades of greys, which are made from mixtures of black and white, if surrounded by, or in juxtaposition with, warm shades of yellowish-red, or red ochres, will appear as refined tones of blue when seen from a distance, as in the case of ceiling decoration.

There are certain colours which "carry" or "read" well at a distance, and others which, however brilliant they may be near at hand, become obscured or indefinite when they are viewed from afar. For example, deep reds, dark blues and greens, intense purples and violets, all become either much darker, or are changed into dirty browns when seen far off, though they may all appear very brilliant when seen near to. Such colours have all low degrees of luminosity, and therefore do not reflect sufficient white light to enable them to carry well. It follows from this that if they were made lighter by the addition of white their carrying powers would be considerably increased, though at a loss of their intensity. The colours that carry, or tell at a distance, in addition to the pale shades of the above-mentioned ones, are the yellows and red ochres, white, buff, emerald green, and cerulean blue.

Coloured surfaces under artificial light.—We have already mentioned that it is only very rarely that the decorator is asked to arrange his colour schemes for rooms that are only used when artificially lighted, and also if his colouring has been planned to be seen in daylight, it will almost invariably look well under artificial light, provided that the room is well lighted. It may, however, be of some advantage to consider some of the more important changes and modifications of colour when viewed by artificial light. Such light would be in ordinary cases that of gas or electric lighting, and although the latter is not so deficient in violet and bluish rays as the former, still it has a considerable amount of yellow rays, though not so much of orange-yellow as gaslight. All kinds of artificial light impart some of their yellow to all colours, and while this kind of illumination improves the brilliancy of yellow and yellowish-reds, or of such colours as lie closely to yellow in the chromatic circle, it dulls and saddens blues, bluish-greens, and violet-blues, or in other words, the colours that are more distantly removed from the orange-yellow in the chromatic circle. Blues and bluish-greens suffer most change in artificial light, as they become degraded to duller and greyer shades. Greens become bluish-greens, yellow-greens are not much changed, bluish-greens become more yellowish. Indigo blue changes to greenish grey. Violet becomes purple, and purple much redder. Yellow becomes paler in artificial light, but, on the contrary, orange becomes redder, and all bright reds from vermilion to carmine become still brighter in hue. Brilliant blues, like cobalt and ultramarine, appear more purplish in gaslight. If we wish, therefore, to obtain a tint of blue that will look blue by gaslight, it must appear as a slightly greenish shade of blue by daylight, and must not be dark in tone. On Plate 13 there are shown a few colours on the left of the diagram, at A, and the approximate changes in these colours, at B, when seen in artificial light.

**Plate 13.—Approximate Change in Certain Colours
when seen in Artificial Light.**

(Under A are certain colours as viewed in daylight. Under B are
similar colours which illustrate the tendency of change of hue
when the former are seen in artificial light)

CHAPTER VI

ITALIAN DECORATION AND ORNAMENT

FROM the twelfth to the end of the sixteenth century was a long period of artistic activity in Italy, when nearly every building, public and private, sacred and secular, was decorated in colour, with paintings and ornament on walls, ceilings and other surfaces, and further enriched with sculpture, and carving in wood, stone or metal. Italian decorative art has in the past so influenced and modified the native art of France, Germany and England, and its influence being still felt and expressed in much of our modern decoration, that an apology is hardly needed if we devote the present chapter to some consideration of the architectural colouring and ornament of the Italian Renaissance.

Apart from the great frescoes and mosaics of the Italian churches and palaces, where pictorial compositions, or decorative pictures, with or without architectural or landscape backgrounds, give the required colour finish to buildings, there exists the very important class of carved, painted, or inlaid ornamentation; though in a measure secondary in the scale of art to the best examples of figure composition, it is in no way, when appropriately designed and applied, inferior as legitimate material for the proper decoration of a building.

The Italians made great use of both carved and painted ornament, which was usually well designed, and in their best work it was employed in a restrained sense as to quantity; the colour and distribution of it, whether in the flat, or in relief, enhanced the beauty of their architecture by assisting, but in no way disturbing, the architectural repose of the building.

The Italian artists of the twelfth and thirteenth centuries used coloured ornament, both of the geometrical and floral varieties, largely in friezes, bands and borders, as a rich kind of framing to enclose, and also to separate, panels which contained their figure compositions, and these ornamental framings were extremely valuable as contrasting foils to the more pictorial compositions which they enclosed. In some cases the ornament itself occupied even as much, and sometimes more, space on the curved and flat surfaces, such as domes, spandrels, panels, and walls, as the figures themselves. A good example of this may be seen in the mosaics of the semi-dome of San Clemente at Rome and also on that of the Church of St. Maria Maggiore, both of which are examples of decoration which are in singular and good harmony with the architecture of the respective churches. We see in this ornament of the twelfth century on the semi-dome of San Clemente a specimen of that variety which was developed, with some modifications, by Cimabue, Torriti,

Giotto, and other Italian artists in the thirteenth and fourteenth centuries.

Plate 14.—Model of Chapel of St. Catherine in the Church of St. Maurizo, Milan. Victoria and Albert Museum.

Plate 15.—Mosaic Decoration: Church of St. John Lateran, Rome.
By Jacopo Torriti. 1287-1292.

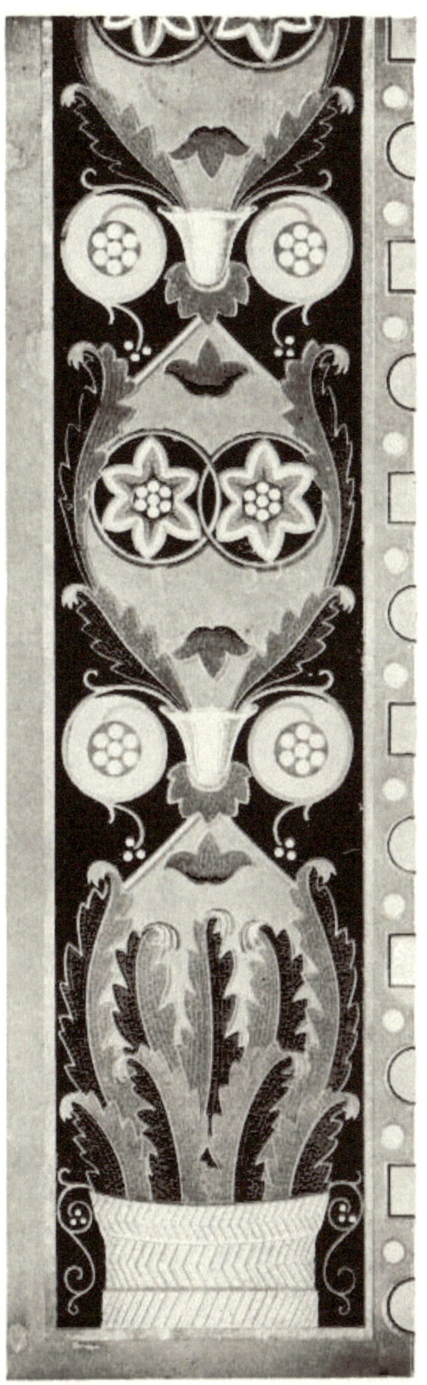

Plate 16.—Portion of the Ornament in Mosaic of the Window Reveals:
Church of St. John Lateran, Rome: 1287-1292.

The particular class of ornament we have now to examine was mainly founded on Roman work, but in addition it was mixed with some geometrical forms, which in the painted variety were copied from the inlaid marble decorations and mosaic patterns of earlier times, and in these geometrical patterns, as well as in some of the floriated scroll-work, derived from early Roman sources, there may be detected a strong influence of Persian or Eastern design. (Plate 16.) It may be said that in all flat ornament used in the decoration of buildings of the thirteenth and fourteenth centuries in Italy, either in painting, mosaic, or inlaid work, Byzantine, Saracenic, or Persian influences may be noticed. This is apparent in the geometrical interlacings, and also in the more natural floral and foliage forms of Western design, where we see strong reflections of certain types of the flat variety of ornament, which is common in the decoration of tiles, pottery, carpets, and other textiles of Asiatic countries.

The Romanesque variety of ornament may be seen in the bands, friezes and borders which frame the paintings attributed to Cimabue in the upper church of St. Francesco at Assisi, and around most of the frescoes by Giotto in the same church.

The drawings on Plate 16, from the mosaics of the window reveals in the Church of St. John, Lateran, by Torriti, illustrate the type of ornament that was common in the thirteenth and first half of the fourteenth centuries. Plate 15 shows the position this ornament occupied in the window reveals, below the semi-dome, and how well it serves as a contrasting division between the figures of the Apostles on the wall spaces between the windows. Here the ornament plays a most effective decorative rôle in combination with the figure subjects of the tribune, and goes to prove that Torriti was fully sensible of the value of ornamental contrast in decorative mosaic, and that he was further aided in obtaining the desired unity of effect by his proper use of colour and simplicity of execution. This work testifies that Torriti was a master in the science of decoration, as he applied the true principles of his art with a correct and profound judgment, and is therefore worthy to be classed among the great forerunners of the Renaissance, and of modern art.

About the beginning of the fourteenth century, when Italy was in a highly prosperous condition, numerous churches, civic and private palaces, guild houses and merchants' houses were erected, most of which were of magnificent proportions, and were richly decorated with sculptured marbles, frescoes, and other ornamentation. The civic palaces and merchants' houses generally presented a solid and massive appearance, the style of architecture, especially in Florence and Central Italy, being a sort of mixture of Romanesque and Gothic styles, the latter being expressed in the window-heads, doorways, lower arcading, and in other details. The massive appearance of the façades were somewhat lightened by the battlements of the top storey and by the boldly projecting cornices and string-courses under them, and under the windows. These projecting features sometimes took the form of a gallery carried on brackets or corbels, between which the machicolations appeared. Types of these civic palaces with their elegant and lofty towers are seen in the Palazzo Vecchio at Florence, and the Palazzo Publico at Siena. Many castle-like guild houses of the fourteenth century are still in existence in Florence and in other cities of Italy, and representations of such may be seen pictured in the frescoes of Giotto at Assisi, and in paintings by other artists in Florence and Siena, where the interiors, with their furniture and decorations, as well as the exteriors are represented. The ceilings of the rooms in these houses were generally flat, or coffered between the beams, or the flat ceiling was often painted to represent coffered panelling. The walls were sometimes painted from the floor up to the dividing line of the deep frieze with imitations of textile hangings, decorated with geometrical patterns of a severe design, heraldic devices, or conventional flowers and foliage. These imitation hangings were represented as suspending from a horizontal rod, hanging perfectly straight, or in some cases from fixed points at regular intervals so as to give them a festoon-like appearance. This was a common method of decorating the lower wall space of house and palace interiors, as well as of churches and chapels. A good illustration of this method of decoration is seen in the Sistine Chapel in the Vatican, where the lower walls under the frescoes of Pinturrichio, Botticelli, C. Rosselli, Perugino, and others are decorated with painted imitations of tapestry hangings. The friezes of the old houses under notice were very important features in the decoration, and were as a rule extremely beautiful in design and colour, the designs usually consisting of a row of fruit trees, such as the orange, lemon, pomegranate, apple, etc., alternating, and placed behind and above a net-work fence, which usually divided the lower wall decoration from the frieze proper, while between the trees, and at the bottom appeared groups of gay flowers, and singing birds at intervals helped to enliven the scene. The friezes often represented stately gardens or orchards, painted in the lively colours of nature, with the backgrounds behind the trees and flowers in black, and the spaces between a deep vermilion red. In some cases the garden frieze was continuous, and complete in itself, and other examples, as in the wall decoration from an old house formerly in the Mercato Vecchio, and now in the monastery of San Marco at Florence, the trees were placed under Gothic canopies, with little towers between, or in arcading supported by pillars, above which were triangular panels filled with heraldic devices. Some of the wall decorations of these old houses had other schemes of diaper-like ornamentation, consisting of lozenge-shaped and foiled figures interlacing at the angles, some spaces being occupied by figures of ladies on horseback, and others by various kinds of birds grouped in landscapes, while the alternating spaces were occupied by circles containing shields with heraldic devices, and around these foliated ornament. The general colour scheme of the walls, frieze, and ceiling was daring, yet delightful. It consisted of a warm harmony of strong reds, black, various greens, golden yellows and russets, modified here and there by the introduction of pearly greys, umber tones, and mellowed white. Rooms decorated in this fashion would be very sumptuous and rich, and would not require the aid of pictures to help out the colour scheme. (Plate 18.) A satisfactory finish to such apartments was admirably achieved by the furniture of the period, which consisted of beautiful Cassoni, in carved or inlaid woods, or decorated in gesso-work, painted and gilded, with representations of lively scenes of the tournament, of hunting and hawking parties, and other romantic subjects. The chairs, the seats against the walls, and the table were of carved walnut, chestnut or cypress wood. If we add to these such accessories as Majolica dishes of lustred pottery, copper and brass vessels, Venetian glass and Oriental carpets, we may conceive some idea of the magnificent effect that a reception-room must have presented in one of these old Florentine houses in the fourteenth and fifteenth centuries.

Plate 17.—Italian Gothic Decoration in the Church of St. Anastasia at Verona.

Plate 18.—Decoration of a Portion of one of the Rooms in the Macchiavelli
Palace, Florence. From a Model in the Victoria and Albert Museum.

Plate 19.—Portion of a Coloured Ceiling (Coved-Ceiling) Decoration by Giulio Romano, in the Palazzo Vecchio at Mantua. Sixteenth Century.

In the charming medley of forms and colour which the wall decorations of these houses presented we may clearly see the development of Giotto's Italian Gothic ornament, still mixed with some of the older Romanesque forms that Torriti loved to use, and while Saracenic influences are not absent, the chief element of beauty in the mixture is the definite expression of natural form and colour, obtained by the trees, flowers, and birds which are introduced in such a dignified manner that they harmonise perfectly with the severer forms of the ornament to which they are allied.

It is to be regretted that this interesting class of ornament was not more fully developed in the fifteenth and sixteenth centuries alongside, if not instead of, the less virile but more classical type which was adopted and developed by Raffaelle and his pupils, Giovanni da Udine, Giulio Romano, and Perina del Vaga, when they came to decorate the Loggie of the Vatican, the interiors of the "Villa Madama," Palazzo del Tè, the Ducal Palace at Mantua (Plates 19 and 20), and the Castello Sant' Angelo at Rome.

In the early years of the sixteenth century excavations were being made at San Pietro in Vincoli and among the ruins of the Palace of Titus, in hopes, as Vasari states, of finding antique statues, when certain subterranean chambers were discovered that were decorated with small "grottesche," so called because they were found in these grottos, or underground chambers; some of the latter were evidently the bathrooms of the palace. Other examples of this kind of decoration were found in the Coliseum, and in the Baths of Diocletian at Rome. Some of these ancient Roman grotesques were modelled in stucco in very low relief, and others were painted, having subjects of mythological figures, amorini, stories, and ornament. (Plate 21.) Raffaelle and his pupil Giovanni da Udine went to see these works, and were so astonished with their novelty, freshness and beauty that they resolved to imitate or adapt them for the decoration of the Loggie of the Vatican. Thus Raffaelle and Giovanni first conceived the idea of a *risorgimento*, a resurrection as well as a revival of these antique forms of decoration, and adopted the scheme and style of ornamentation for the piers, pilasters, arches and friezes of the Vatican Loggie. The painted portion of the pilasters have elaborate scroll-work, based on acanthus foliage, with designs consisting of fruit, flowers, trees, birds, quadrupeds, human figures, and enlarged copies of antique gems and bas-reliefs in panels surrounded by decorated mouldings, all in a rich scheme of polychromy on cream-coloured grounds. The vaulted ceilings of the Loggie are divided into compartments having stucco mouldings, some of which contain painted figure subjects, and others are executed in low-relief stucco work. The decorations of the lower parts are now, however, in a bad state, being mostly perished or rubbed off, but those of the ceilings and arches are in a fairly good condition.

In some of the apartments of the Popes, in the Castello Sant' Angelo at Rome, there are many examples of this kind of decoration, executed by Da Udine, Giulio Romano and Perina del Vaga, among which may be mentioned the beautiful little bathroom, the walls and ceiling of which are entirely covered with arabesques and grotesques, in colour on a white ground, which Giovanni da Udine painted for Pope Leo.

Plate 20.—Arabesque Decorations in the Ducal Palace, Mantua.
By Giulio Romano. Sixteenth Century.

The "Villa Madama," near Rome, was built, or finished about 1521, from designs by Raffaelle, a year or so after his death, and the interior was decorated by

Giovanni da Udine, chiefly in stucco, or *gesso duro*, in the same manner as the work in the Vatican Loggie. The decorated portion of this villa is chiefly confined to the great Loggia and its vestibule, and the two square recesses between them. The Loggia is divided into three bays, the centre one having a domed roof, while the other two have vaulted roofs, each roof being divided into four segments. The designs on the piers are executed in *gesso duro*, and consist of conventional renderings of the vine, maple, and other plants, admirable in conception and skilful in technique. This work, together with the relief decorations of the circular vaulting of the recesses, and soffits of the arches, is left uncoloured. Colour is used sparingly amongst the high reliefs which cover the greater part of the central dome. There are four panels in this dome with paintings of the figures of Neptune, Jupiter, Juno and Plato which are attributed to Giulio Romano. The groin ceiling-ribs of the right and left bays are painted with bands of arabesques and foliage designs, and the surfaces of the vaults are richly decorated with coloured ornaments. In the centre of each of these four vault divisions there is a large oval panel, one set of four having groups of sporting amorini, and the other four have mythological subjects. The three recesses have similar decorations. Much of the painting has suffered from damp, and wet from the roof, but in the better preserved remains of the painted work, and of the stucco decorations, there is sufficient evidence left to justify the great praise that Vasari has bestowed upon it, for on the whole it is more refined in design and execution than Giovanni's early work in the Loggie of the Vatican. Similar kind of stucco decoration may be seen on the richly ornamented columns of the courtyard in the Palazzo Vecchio, at Florence, and similar painted arabesques on the vaulted ceilings and arch soffits of the same courtyard, though now much decayed and darkened by age and weather.

In the Ducal Palace at Mantua are three celebrated "Camerini," or apartments of Isabella d'Este, who became Marchioness of Mantua by her marriage in 1490 with the Marquis Giovanni Francesco Gonzaga. These rooms are in the part of the palace known as the "Paradiso," and were beautifully decorated by the best known artists of the period to the orders of the Marchioness. The first of the three apartments was the music-room, the walls of which were lined with "intarsia" of different coloured woods representing views of towns. The ceiling was panelled and decorated with ornament and heraldic devices in low relief, and the frieze was formed of musical instruments carved in the wood. The second apartment was the painting-room, which from the point of decorative beauty was the most important of the three. Its chief interest consisted in the six pictures which Isabella had painted to her orders by Mantegna, Lorenzo Costa, Perugino, and Bellini. These famous pictures, with the exception of the one painted by the last-named artist, which cannot be traced, were taken from their places on the walls of the room, and sold by Prince Vincenzo Gonzaga in 1627 to Cardinal Richelieu, and were afterwards bought from the heirs of the Cardinal by the French Government, and are now in the Louvre at Paris. A model of one side of this beautiful "Camerino," two-thirds of its actual size, with copies of the three allegorical pictures which once adorned its walls, together with the richly carved candelabra-like pillars that separated the pictures, a portion of the frieze and panelled ceiling in gold and blue, with the marble doorway by Cristoforo Romano is now in the Victoria and Albert Museum, and another copy is in the Dublin National Museum. The third apartment was reserved for receptions and was decorated with delicately carved devices, mottoes, and the heraldic arms of the family, executed in wood-carving and stucco finished in gold and having a blue background. The celebrated pictures that originally adorned the walls of the painting-room are elaborately finished and highly imaginative works, and are therefore to be regarded more as easel paintings than decorative compositions. This small room, which measures only seventeen feet by ten feet, must have appeared, in its original state, a veritable cabinet of the finest art and craftsmanship of the Renaissance period.

Mantua is very rich in the work of Giulio Romano (1492-1546) and of his pupils, Primaticcio and Niccolo dell' Abbate; the two latter with Serlio, the architect, were chiefest among the many Italian artists and craftsmen who were summoned to Fontainebleau by the French King, François I, and were in a great measure responsible for the spread of the Italian influences which were so apparent in the art of the early French Renaissance.

Plate 21.—Coloured Decoration of Portion of a Coved Ceiling in the Vatican.
By Raffaelle. Sixteenth Century.

Giulio Romano settled in Mantua in 1524, when he was employed by Federico II to alter and decorate some of the rooms in the Ducal Palace. He was also the architect and decorator of the Palazza del Tè, the country house of Federico, near Mantua. The paintings executed on the walls of these palaces by Giulio Romano and his pupils, Primaticcio, Francesco Penni, Rinaldo of Mantua, and Niccolo dell' Abbate, consist chiefly of mythological subjects, and historical events from classic literature, battles of giants, gladiatorial combats, market-place, seaside and fishing scenes, with occasional subjects from the Old Testament, all of which were painted in the vigorous style and strong colouring so characteristic of Romano's work. On the other hand, there were many cabinets and apartments in these palaces that were richly decorated with beautiful designs in stucco-work and fanciful arabesques, painted in colours and in monochrome, with great brilliancy and freedom, refined in conception, with lightness of touch in the execution, and not wanting in the frank gaiety of colour expression. This kind of relief and painted decoration occurs mostly on the vaulted and coved ceilings, on soffits of the arches, in spandrels, and on numerous borders, friezes and pilasters. (Plate 21.) The purely arabesque ornamentation usually occupied the large spaces on ceilings and elsewhere that surround the central oval, circular or rectangular panels which often contained figure-subjects of a mythological character, or sometimes heads, busts, or devices of various kinds, and usually consists of scroll-like foliage of vines and other plants, interspersed with sporting amorini, birds, and other creatures (Fig. 21), precisely a reflex of the grottesche decorations of the Roman Imperial times, except that such painted Italian arabesques of Raffaelle's time, and later, would be more often, in the earlier Roman period, modelled in very low stucco-relief, for the ancients used their magnificent stucco composition to a far greater extent in decoration than the Renaissance artists, whether it was afterwards coloured or not.

It will be seen that all this kind of decoration, whether ancient or modern, painted or modelled, was entirely an applied decoration, and therefore non-constructional; that is to say, the ornamentation was applied to large surfaces of walls, ceilings, piers and pilasters, etc., after the building was completed. The decoration was added, and did not grow out of the structure, and was therefore unlike the Egyptian, Greek, Persian, Arabian, Medieval Gothic, and much of the Byzantine decoration, which grew out of the structure, as an inevitable growth, and which would be illogical and incongruous if applied to any other style of architecture than the particular style that had given birth to it.

The case is different in the applied decoration of the Roman and Pompeian houses, baths and grottos, and in the Renaissance adaptation of this kind of adornment, which does not appear to be strictly connected with the architecture. Similarly shaped spaces, for example, are found to be decorated in many different ways, some vaulted ceilings are covered with elaborate scroll-work, others are divided into panels of various shapes having stucco mouldings planted on the walls surrounding them, or dividing all forms of space divisions. Wall spaces are decorated in the Roman examples, but more especially in Pompeian decoration, without much regard to the wall as an architectural feature, for we find superimposed forms of thin columns, supporting fantastical and impossible entablatures, curtains, festoons, scroll-work, landscapes, figure subjects, animals, and all kinds of arbitrary spacings. It must be said, however, that if this applied decoration is unconnected with the building, it is very interesting and often charming in its spontaneity of colour and form, while the beauty and refined technique of the low-relief figure and animal forms go a long way to counterbalance the illogical nature of the general surface adornment.

CHAPTER VII
COLOURED ARCHITECTURE IN FRANCE

IN France the traditional custom of colouring as applied to the exteriors of buildings was continued and maintained throughout the Middle Ages and the Renaissance period, but it had gradually declined in the reign of Louis XIII (1610-42), and was practically non-existent in the time of Louis XIV. In the Gallo-Roman era public buildings and monuments in France were coloured inside and out. Gregory of Tours (539-93), and Frodoard (894-966) make mention of churches and palaces that were decorated with paintings in their time. The Church of Saint-Savin, near Poitiers, dating from 1023, has the oldest monumental paintings in France, which were executed a little after the church was built. The façade of Notre Dame in Paris still bears slight traces of painting. According to Viollet-le-Duc's researches the three doors with their arches and tympana were painted and gilded, also the niches, the "galerie-des-Rois," the arcades under the tower, and the great central rose of the façade were all "radiant with bright colour and gilding." This colouring occurred principally on the mouldings, columns, sculptured ornament and figure work. The outside colouring was much more vivid than the inside work. There were bright reds, crude greens, orange, yellow ochre, blacks and pure whites, but rarely blues, outside, the brilliancy of light allowing a harshness of colouring that would not be tolerable under the diffused light of the interior. The large gables of the transept also bear traces of old painting. There is also evidence that the greater portion of similar edifices of the thirteenth, fourteenth and fifteenth centuries, in France, were decorated in colour.

Enamelled tiles, pottery plaques and gilded leadwork were largely used at the beginning of the Renaissance. Enamelled pottery and terra-cotta decoration were introduced into France by Girolamo della Robbia, who was invited in company with Primaticcio, Serlio and many other Italian artists by François I. Girolamo decorated the Château-de-Boulogne with glazed earthenware; this building was demolished in 1792, and some of the earthenware plaques are now in the Cluny Museum at Paris. During the reigns of François I and Henri II, in the sixteenth century, the architectural colouring was mostly a development of that of the Middle Ages, but towards the end of the century the taste for colour decoration rapidly declined, and from the beginning of the reign of Louis XIV the marble, and cold white stone style of building, introduced from Italy, became the fashion in France. This applies more particularly to the exteriors of French edifices, for during the reign of the Grand Roi the interiors continued to have a goodly share of coloured decorative paintings.

In the "Louis-Quinze" period (1715-74) colour was still used, but more sparingly, on the exterior and interior of buildings. Some ceilings and doorhead panels were painted in colours, but as a rule white relieved with gold was the common scheme of decoration, or sometimes pale and weak tints of colour were used.

In the period of the "Louis-Seize" style (1774-92), the schemes of decoration were almost as colourless as in the former period, although some exceptions must be noted, as in the case of some exquisitely decorated boudoirs painted for Marie Antoinette and her ladies of the court, examples of which are the Queen's boudoir at Fontainebleau, and one which was formerly that of one of her maids-of-honour, a beautiful specimen of its kind, which is now in the Victoria and Albert Museum at South Kensington. (Plates 22 and 23.) From the days of the Republic to the end of Napoleon's reign, 1792-1814, the architecture and decoration became still more cold and austere, and except in isolated instances there was not much employment of colour to relieve the conventional formality of the so-called "Empire" style.

The Romantic School of artists, poets, and historians was ushered in after the Revolution of 1830, when greater attention was paid to the interesting works in art and literature of the Middle Ages and of the Renaissance, and one of the consequences of this great movement was the revival of colour decoration on buildings. Many old frescoes which had been covered with whitewash, not only in France, but in Germany, in the Rhine valley, and in England also, were once more brought to light, after the whitewash of previous centuries had been removed. Many French architects, artists, and archæologists, among whom were Prosper Merimée, Didron, and Viollet-le-Duc, advocated a more generous use of colour, not only in the interiors, but on the exteriors of buildings. Many works on ancient art were published about this time, which also contributed to the education of the public taste, and French architects and students were becoming enthusiasts for the application of deep colouring to architecture, being led in this direction by the discoveries of Hittorf, in 1823, and subsequently by others, who went out to Greece and Sicily and found traces of strong colouring on the ancient Greek temples at Segesta and Selinus in Sicily. Hittorf was the first to discover and make known the ancient polychromy of the Greeks. The traces of colouring which he found on the three temples near the Acropolis of Selinus, and those on the small temple of Empedocles at the same place, enabled him to restore the colouring of these buildings, and in 1851 he published his work, entitled *L'Architecture Polychrôme chez les Grecs*, and also a view of the great Temple of Jupiter. About the same time the sculptor Thorwaldsen also found numerous traces of blue, red, and gold on the Temple of Ægina. Hittorf's discoveries of Greek colouring were at first received in France with a good deal of scepticism and violent opposition, as he was told that the colouring of the Sicilian temples was only the remains of "the vulgar daubing of Byzantine, Norman, or Arab origin." It is now, however, clearly proved by the light of subsequent investigations that Greek polychromy was a tradition of the colouring of still older temples, and that the latter was only a development of the archaic polychromy of the primitive Mycenian decorators, who in their turn derived it from Egyptian sources.

Plate 22.—Decoration of the Boudoir of Madame de Serilly,
now in the Victoria and Albert Museum. French, Eighteenth Century.

[Victoria and Albert Museum.

Plate 23.—Another Portion of the Decoration of the Boudoir of Madame de Serilly: French, Eighteenth Century.

About the middle of the nineteenth century the art of colour decoration on buildings was greatly advanced, as the public were becoming familiarised with ancient work by means of copies made of it, illustrated books, and photographs of Pompeian, Roman, Greek, Byzantine, Persian, Egyptian, Eastern and Italian Renaissance work. The decoration of buildings in France in the nineteenth century in respect to the revival of polychromy may therefore be looked upon as a veritable colour renaissance, for a reaction had set in against the almost colourless buildings of the two former centuries. Not only was colour extensively employed in the interiors of French buildings, but on the exteriors it was used in a structural sense by the employment of natural coloured materials, such as marbles, bronze, terra-cotta and enamelled earthenware, and by the applied decoration of mosaic.

The architects, Duban and Labrouste, were among the first to assist in the creation of this new taste for colour, they having thoroughly studied the remains of Greek and Roman architecture, and especially the colour decoration of Pompeii. Duban set about the work of restoring the colour decorations of the Sainte Chapelle, in Paris, and those of the Chateau-de-Blois, where in the latter he used ceramic tiles successfully in the decoration, taking his models from the tile work of the Middle Ages. Other works done by Duban, or under his directions, were the restoration of the Galerie-du-Louvre in the painted "loge" and decorated ceiling, and at the École des Beaux-Arts, the "Loggie-di-Rafaele," in the galleries of the first storey, and the porticoes in the Cour-du-Murier, which he decorated in the Pompeian style. Duban employed marble, enamelled pottery, terra-cotta and iron, as well as paint, for his decorative colour schemes.

Many architects and artists were very enthusiastic about this time in advocating the extended use of colour on buildings, and numerous old churches and chateaux were restored to their former colouring, but those who undertook such work were not all gifted as colourists, and consequently some mistakes and failures happened; but at the same time a considerable amount of good work was accomplished where refined excellence and harmonious expression of colour were by no means wanting. Alfred Norman and Louis Duc were successful decorators of this period. Among the works of the former was the beautifully decorated house in the Pompeian style, painted for Louis Napoleon, and the latter architect used glazed tiles in combination with painting in some successful schemes of decoration in the oriental method of colouring. The Church of Saint Germain-des-Prés, in Paris, which contains the frescoes of Hippolyte Flandrin, was admirably decorated by Denuelle under the direction of the architect, Victor Baltard. In connection with the colour revival in France, Viollet-le-Duc makes this reflection: "Why do we deprive ourselves of all these resources of art? Why does the classic school pretend that coldness and monotony are the inseparable accompaniments of beauty, when the Greeks, whom they present to us as artists *par excellence,* always coloured their buildings inside and out, not timidly, but by putting on colours of extreme brilliancy?"

The use of coloured terra-cotta, ceramic tiles and mosaic, rapidly spread in France about this time, for the architects and the public had become acquainted with the coloured tile decoration of Moorish palaces in Spain, the tile facings of mosques in Persia, Cairo, and of the Mohammedan palaces and mosques of India. In conjunction with this kind of decoration, mosaic work also reappeared in France. Charles Garnier, the eminent architect, designed and built the new Opera House in Paris, in the years 1871 and 1872, where he introduced mosaic on a large scale, both inside and outside this important building. He also used mosaics and enamels in the decoration of the Casino at Monte Carlo. The polychromy of the Opera House in Paris is of a refined and dignified character, which, on the exterior of the building, is obtained by marble, bronze, mosaic, enamelled earthenware and gilding, and in the interior by mosaics and the painted decorations of Paul Baudry and other artists. Garnier was an enthusiast in the colouring of architecture, and especially for the use of mosaic in the decoration of buildings. In his dream of the future of Paris, he predicts that "The grounds of the cornices will shine with eternal colours, the piers will be enriched with sparkling panels, gilded friezes will run along the buildings. The monuments will be clothed with marbles and enamels, and mosaics will make all love movement and colour." Garnier brought over to Paris many Italian mosaic workers, and it was largely due to his influence that the Government established the French École de Mosaïque at Sèvres, which has achieved excellent results under the direction of the late M. Gerspach.

Glazed tiles, enamelled earthenware, coloured wood, bronze and mosaic were from this time forward employed as decorative materials in public and private buildings in Paris and throughout the provinces. The great International Exhibitions were in some degree decorated with these materials, and the exhibits of these coloured building materials from England, France itself, and other countries, gave a great impetus to the production of such, especially to those of the potter's art. In France the large decorative panels in coloured tile work by M. Deck created an epoch in this kind of work.

Foremost among the many architects and artists in the advocacy of colour in buildings was the late M. Paul Sédille, whose work in the effective use of enamelled terra-cotta and glass mosaic in decoration is well known in Paris. He designed, among other work, the beautiful monumental doorway as the entrance to the Salle des Beaux-Arts in the Exposition-Universelle of 1878 at Paris, which was composed exclusively of coloured terra-cotta and glazed tiles, similar to that of the Italian "Della Robbia" variety. This enamelled doorway was modelled in relief and painted in contrasting colours of green, red, natural colours, black and white, on pale yellow and azure grounds. The wreaths, stars, palms, and other salient portions of the design were in gold. Another work of his is that of the decoration of the ceiling of the vestibule of the Magazin-du-Printemps in Paris, where he has used enamelled glass mosaic with variegated marbles in an ornamental design, enclosed with plain and gilt bronze mouldings. The colouring of this effective design is very simple but rich, the ground being gold, the foliage pale greens, and the flowers white, slightly shaded with rose colour.

The most important mosaic decoration in France is perhaps that of the apse of the Panthéon at Paris, by the artist M. E. Hébert. The subject of the composition is "Christ revealing to the Angel of France the Destinies of her People." The figure of Christ occupies the centre of the hemispherical vault, and stands before a throne; the right hand is uplifted, and in the left is the rolled volume—the book of the future—sealed with the seven seals. On His right the Virgin presents Joan of Arc with her standard banner, and on the left the Angel of France, whose red wings are heightened with gold, and with sword in hand, presents Sainte Geneviève, of Paris. The ground of the composition is gold. The figure of Christ is clothed in a robe of purple, and has a border of gold, and that of the Virgin is white with a gold fringe. The Angel of France is robed in a rose-coloured garment, and has a bluish-green coloured mantle. St. Geneviève has a blue robe and a grey mantle. All the personages stand on a verdured meadow, which is enamelled with flowers. Elaborate borders of vine leafage and grapes, with fillets of precious stones, surround the composition, which are from the designs of M. Galland, one of the finest decorative artists of France. The composition, character and colouring of this important mosaic, as well as the technique, are based on the best traditions of the Ravenna mosaics of the fifth and sixth centuries.

In the French provinces many examples of colour decoration and mosaic work have been executed in recent years, notably the mosaic decorations of the new cathedrals at Marseilles and Lyons. The municipal buildings of Paris and of the provincial cities of France, together with churches, universities, and other public and private buildings, contain numerous examples of important wall paintings, which though of great interest individually, are rather to be regarded as isolated efforts of decorative or pictorial value than complete schemes of the colour decoration of the buildings which they adorn.

In regard to what we have just said, it will be necessary to make a very important exception in the case of at least one great French master of decorative art, namely, Puvis de Chavannes, for he was perhaps the greatest decorator that France has produced. No one understood so well as he did the laws and principles of architectural decoration and colouring. He was almost alone among the artists of France in his proper treatment of the wall surface as an architectural feature, for on looking at his work one always feels that the wall is in evidence as a solid and flat surface, and that his great pictorial decorations, as far as the design and colouring of them go, and so full of beauty and interest as they are, in no way interfere with the architectural function of the wall. A comparison of his work in the Panthéon at Paris with that of the other artists whose works occupy other wall spaces in that building clearly proves this contention, for, as a rule, the surrounding wall paintings, executed by about ten other artists, though excellent as illustrative works of art, are really out of place as wall decorations in their composition, treatment of design, and more particularly in their violent colouring. They do not harmonise with the dignity of the architecture, they are not legitimate decorations, but rather great pictures fastened to the walls, making a lively and gay picture-gallery in a solemn and dignified building, and lacking that monumental fitness in their design and colouring which is so well expressed in the work of Puvis de Chavannes.

All the painters of these wall pictures in the Panthéon, with the exception of Chavannes, seem to have been influenced by the works of Paul Veronese, Tintoretto, Titian and Rubens, who produced large, and even colossal-sized oil paintings, which were designed to fit wall and ceiling spaces as decorative pictures, and were glorious things in themselves with all their richness of colour, perspective, composition and vigour of brush-work in the execution, but none of them can be considered as suitable decoration of the spaces they occupy on ceilings and walls. The Italian Primitive School, and the great frescanti of Italy, in the fifteenth and sixteenth centuries, understood the requirements of wall decoration much better than the later, though great, Italian and Flemish masters, who painted their pictures chiefly in the oil medium. Chavannes, however, apparently founded his style and methods on the work of the early Italians, and, though he painted in an oil and wax medium on canvas which was "marouflée," or cemented, on to the wall, and not painted on the wall direct, as in fresco or tempera, his work shows strong decorative influences derived from the study of these early Italian masters.

It would not be difficult to point out some of the many instances where the majority of the Panthéon wall pictures fail as decoration, where violent contrasts of colour and extreme perspective effects are, as it would appear, almost aimed for, as if the object was to destroy the plane of the wall as a flat surface, by making it look as if it had holes or windows, rather than any striving for the preservation of its natural solidity.

The wall picture, "Vers La Gloire," by the clever artist, Detaille, may be mentioned as an example of work that has reached the limits of misplaced decoration. This work, though no doubt very popular, is really a crowded and complex miniature painting enlarged and transferred to the wall. In this painting there are represented hundreds of soldiers and horses all in the most violent action, with banners flying, and a plethora of swords, spears and trumpets; the horses are madly galloping on and through the clouds, there is plenty of movement, and great cleverness is displayed in the grouping of the horsemen, but at a few yards' distance the work appears to be a merely glittering and spotty achievement, and when examined closely represents a perfect museum of soldiers' uniforms. Clever as this work is, it is, however, entirely out of place on the walls of the Panthéon, for, apart from the unsuitability of the subject, it cramps and destroys the amplitude, as well as the flatness and solidity of the wall, which should be the first care of the artist to preserve.

The wall paintings in this building by Puvis de Chavannes, in contrast to the works above-mentioned, are designed and executed in a truly decorative sense. Here he has painted a magnificent series of panels illustrating incidents in the life of St. Geneviève, the patron saint of Paris. The general colour of these pastoral works is a combination of grey greens, pale yellows, and pale purples, which produces an atmosphere that is silvery and tender. The compositions are dignified and impressive, and there is no crowding or complexity in the almost even distribution of the figures; the keynote is simplicity, which gives the monumental clearness of design that decorative painting demands. In this respect the work of Chavannes has much in common with the charm and *naïveté* of the work of the Italian Primitives.

At the Hôtel de Ville he has painted the subjects of "L'Hiver," "L'Eté," and "Victor Hugo offrant son Lyre à la Ville de Paris," but perhaps his greatest achievement is his celebrated painting of the "Lettres, Arts et Muses" which decorates the hemicycle of the vast Amphitheatre of the Sorbonne at Paris. The subject was one that was entirely in harmony with the painter's genius and powers. The composition contains forty-four life-sized figures, which are arranged in a series of cleverly designed groups, all connected with each other, and arranged symmetrically, but not with a dry symmetry, on either side of a central group of three figures—Mnemosyne, the mother of the Muses, seated, with boys on either side, who are evidently meant to personify Love and Fame. The other figures symbolise Literature, Art, and Poetry. The background scene is a sacred wood, where the graceful tree trunks are kept rather thin and slender, so as not to interfere with the figures, but these serried rows of trees give the requisite upright lines that steady and strengthen the composition, which is also helped immensely by a dark hedge, extending the whole length of the picture, above which a little sky is shown.

The colour scheme is a beautiful harmony of fairly strong half-tones of such colours as greens, reds, yellows, blues, orange, grey and purple, but as a whole the dominant harmony is that of green and purple, although neither of these colours appears in its full or positive hue. The general colour scheme of this work is unusually intense in comparison with the paler and more tender colouring of the other works of this painter. His figures are types or embodiments of his poetic ideas, for, like Blake and Botticelli, he used the human form in his designs, not in any realistic sense, but as a medium for the expression of his ideas and inward vision; in short, he subordinated form to his thought.

The staircase walls in the Museum at Lyons have been decorated with paintings by Puvis de Chavannes; he is also well represented in his important wall paintings in the museums of Rouen, Marseilles, and Amiens, and his latest work was the decorative paintings in the Library at Boston, in America. Some of his earliest works, and other later ones, are those that form the important wall decorations in the Picardy Museum at Amiens, and this museum affords an excellent opportunity for the student who wishes to study the art of Puvis de Chavannes, for it contains many and typical examples of his design, drawing, composition, and colour. There are some very large paintings of his which decorate the main staircase walls, and there is also here a special gallery devoted to his work, the walls of which are covered by his paintings, all of which are surrounded by richly coloured Pompeian borders and panels of ornament. The architectural mouldings and other features are also richly coloured, and this surrounding colour and ornament does not in any way interfere with the pictorial composition, but, on the other hand, unites the paintings with the architecture, the whole effect providing a fine example of colour finish to the gallery.

Generally speaking, the majority of painters who are called upon to execute wall paintings in public buildings are afraid to use colour or coloured ornament close to, or surrounding, their pictorial compositions; but the best Italian artists, and the Greeks also, invariably did surround their decorative pictures with coloured geometric patterns, and coloured the architectural mouldings as well. So when we find such a great decorator as Chavannes adopting the principle of using colour to aid the effect of his decorative picture, and thus following the practice of the old masters, we may be assured that ornamental bands, lines, and mouldings, if coloured in harmony with the pictorial compositions, will effectively assist the latter in their function of providing a true decoration of the building, and prevent them from having the isolated appearance of pictures fastened on the walls.

CHAPTER VIII

COLOUR DECORATION IN GERMANY

THERE was little, if any, art or architecture in Germany before the days of Charlemagne, except that which found expression in the various articles and objects of personal adornment, such as in brooches, rings, in the costume of the warriors and chiefs, and in some objects of general utility, where the lesser arts—*die Kleinkünste*—were developed and attained to high degrees of perfection, in the Romanesque period and Middle Ages. Charlemagne, who reigned from 768 to 814, was a great art-loving prince, and gave the first impulse to art in Germany when he built his stately church, which he also intended for his tomb, at Aachen (Aix-la-Chapelle). Here he had also his chief palace, but of this, and of the many others he possessed on the banks of the Rhine, no definite traces remain but his palace-chapel, now the cathedral, or the round portion of the latter, which still exists in good preservation, and is a fitting monument to his greatness, and to his zeal for the promotion of art in Germany. This church is said to be a copy in plan of the Byzantine Church of St. Vitale at Ravenna, except that the latter is an octagon in the ground plan, and the former is a polygon of sixteen sides. This round type of building was used in Rome and the south not only for churches, but for baptisteries, and after Charlemagne's Chapel was erected in Aachen it became the prototype of circular churches that were built in the Romanesque period and style in Germany. The church at Aix-la-Chapelle was decorated with mosaics, similar to those of St. Vitale at Ravenna, but the original mosaics have all perished, and the ones which now adorn the dome and pendentives of the church are modern works by Salviati of Venice, and were executed from a seventeenth-century copy of the old mosaic. The subject of the dome mosaic, on a gold ground, represents Christ and the twenty-four Elders of the Apocalypse. The rest of the central part of the church, ambulatory walls, etc., are adorned with mosaics within the last ten years. The choir of this interesting church is an addition, and is a Gothic building of the fifteenth century. Its walls and vaulted ceiling are richly adorned with ornamentation in colours and gold, the patterns of the ornament being similar to, or derived from, the silk tapestries of that period.

Mosaic as church decoration, except for floor pavements, was not much in use in Germany after the time of Charlemagne; in the northern countries of Europe wall painting in tempera became the characteristic method of decoration for the Romanesque churches, just as mosaic was the chief kind of decoration for churches in Italy and southern Europe in the same period.

In the Romanesque epoch in Germany, the period which is generally understood to extend from A.D. 1000 till about 1200, or a little later, no church was without its painted decoration. The subjects were similar to, and the general design and style of drawing were not unlike the mosaic decoration of churches in Italy and Sicily. Single figures, and scenes from the Old and New Testaments were enclosed in panels, having borders designed in elaborate ornamental forms, derived chiefly from conventional leafage. The figures were usually painted in flat tints, or almost so; very little shading or modelling of the forms were attempted, and the whole work was strongly outlined, so that the finished decoration appeared as an enlarged kind of illumination. The ribs or groups of mouldings of the vaulted ceilings and the soffits of the arches were decorated with conventional flowers, garlands and ribbon work. The apse usually contained a large figure of Christ, or the Madonna enthroned, surrounded with figures of the Apostles and Saints, and often on the other parts of the church, such as the triumphal arch, the ceilings and walls, there were paintings representing the visions of the Prophets, and the imaginative imagery of the Apocalypse.

The Romanesque churches of the Rhineland afford many examples of interior colour decoration, for it was in the region watered by the Rhine that German art was cradled, where it was carefully nursed, and where it developed to an early maturity. Mural painting as a handmaid, or as an auxiliary to Romanesque architecture, can still be studied in many of the old churches in the valley of the Rhine, where it was an important art as early as the eleventh century. The secular buildings also, such as the castles, guild-houses, town-halls, chateaux and private houses were all at this time decorated in colour, but nearly all of their colour decorations and paintings have been destroyed in the course of time, except some remaining fragments which have been removed to local museums. There are, however, a few churches of the Romanesque period that still have a considerable amount of the eleventh and twelfth century paintings on their walls, and though much of this work is greatly faded and has now very little of its former colour and beauty, yet the composition and outlines are still in evidence, and although we cannot well judge of their original colouring there are still much quaintness and charm attached to those examples which have not yet been restored.

There are four Romanesque churches of the Rhine valley which still have their wall paintings of the eleventh and twelfth centuries, namely, the double church at Schwarz Rheindorf, near Bonn, with paintings that were originally executed about 1150, the chapter-house of the Abbey-church at Brauweiler, near Cologne, and the crypt of St. Maria im Capitol at Cologne. The baptistery of the Church of St. Gereon has some wall paintings of the thirteenth century, and still older work in the crypt.

Perhaps the most important and most interesting of these old wall-paintings are those that adorn the lower church at Schwarz Rheindorf, although they have been completely repainted recently, but it must be admitted the present colouring of them is characteristic of the Romanesque colour, and can hardly be very far wrong. The subjects appear to be highly imaginative and poetical conceptions of Biblical scenes, and there are large figures of the Apostles and Hebrew prophets. The treatment is in the usual flat method of colouring with strong outlines. The original paintings were discovered under coats of whitewash in 1853. The Chapter-house at Brauweiler has some examples of wall-paintings, dating from the end of the twelfth century, the subjects being scenes from the Epistle to the Hebrews. In the apse of the church there are other paintings of the later Gothic period.

In the crypt of the Church of St. Maria im Capitol, at Cologne, there are some interesting wall paintings of the twelfth century, but they are in a faded state. This church, however, is remarkable for its rich modern colouring, and furnishes one of the best examples of the revival of Romanesque decoration in Germany. It may be said that every inch of the surfaces of the interior is covered with richly-coloured ornamentation and figure-paintings, which includes the columns and piers. The east end is in plan trefoil-like, having three semicircles with their diameters touching, and the three semi-domes above have figure subjects that were designed, and the painting begun, by Steinle, but finished by other artists.

In the crypt of the Church of St. Gereon at Cologne there is a very interesting series of wall paintings, consisting of single figures of a colossal size, each painted in curved recesses in the walls. The figures are noble in design, but the colouring is much faded. They date from about the twelfth century, and appear to be examples of the original work, that have not been restored. It may be mentioned here that the floor of the crypt is a mosaic pavement of the eleventh century. It is Roman in character, though of German workmanship. The design consists of figure subjects, where David, Samson, and Delilah are represented, and also the signs of the Zodiac. These mosaic pavements were discontinued after the eleventh century, when encaustic and glazed tiles of brown, red or green colours were used instead of mosaic for floor pavements. The walls of the baptistery of this church are decorated with painted figures, of thirteenth-century work. Full length figures of saints and warriors are arranged in pairs, two of them occupying the upper half of each arched bay between engaged pillars, and between each two figures is a small painted column. The lower halves of the bays have each an ornamental border immediately under each pair of figures, and the rest of the space below the border is painted in imitation of suspended tapestries. Altogether this makes a very satisfactory and interesting scheme of decoration. Such schemes were very common in the decoration of the Gothic period in Germany and other countries. The rest of the interior of this church, like that of St. Maria im Capitol, is lavishly decorated in richly-coloured and gold ornamentation being a modern revival of Romanesque colouring. The profuse surface decoration used so much in the Romanesque period was of Byzantine origin, and consisted of an almost endless variety of forms and motives, such as conventional vine leafage, fruit and tendrils, flowers of various kinds, scale patterns, interlacings, frets, geometrical combinations, chevrons, zigzag patterns, ribbons, garlands, and various representations of carved Byzantine ornament, and other architectural features, such as arcading, all treated flatly in colour.

There are other numerous examples of Romanesque painting, colouring and ornamental decoration still found in other parts of Germany, besides the examples we have just noticed. The walls and ceilings of the choir and transepts of Brunswick Cathedral have a complete series of Romanesque wall paintings of the twelfth century. The finest example of this style of painting in Germany is the magnificent ceiling of the great nave of St. Michael's Church in Hildesheim. It is a flat ceiling of wooden construction. Running the whole length of the central portion of the ceiling the space is subdivided into a series of square panels; on each side of this central space the bands are divided into a great many small oblong panels, and outside these is a broad enclosing border of scroll-work containing in circular spaces in this border half-length figures of saints. The adjoining border has its oblong panels filled with small full-length figures of Apostles and Prophets. The larger square panels of the central part have lozenges and quatrefoil forms inside each square, in alternation. The latter forms contain the seated figures of kings and other personages that illustrate the genealogy of Christ, or the Root of Jesse. The Fall is also represented, and the corner spaces outside the lozenges and quatrefoils are filled with ornament and small medallions that add great richness to the design without giving to it any appearance of confusion. The colour is very strong and rich, and the whole of the decoration is painted on a blue ground.

The small stained-glass windows of the Romanesque period add a further note of colour to the interiors, although coloured glass was quite secondary to the painted decoration of this time. The only figure-work attempted in the glass was that in the small circular medallions and lozenge-shaped panels, containing scriptural subjects, which were placed at intervals amidst a rich setting of leaf patterns and other ornamental forms.

In the Gothic period, from the twelfth to the fourteenth centuries, when the walls of churches became less in extent and area, and the windows became larger and more numerous, glass painting gradually became the chief factor in providing the colour of church interiors, and consequently the art and craft of the glass painter or "glazier," as he was called in the old documents, became a more important one than that of the painter and decorator. When the Gothic builders perfected the rib vaulting system, their greatest discovery, and the keynote of the style, they found that walls were not necessary as active agents of the construction, but of use only in filling up the spaces between the voids, and were therefore more or less inert masses. They found that they had no use for walls except to close in the building from the weather, and so we find that walls began to disappear in Gothic buildings, and the windows being more numerous and larger, the Gothic churches were becoming great glasshouses. To prevent this look it was necessary to fill the windows with coloured glass, which subdued the otherwise great glare of white light that would come through clear glass, and would give the interiors a more comfortable appearance, at the same time adding colour decoration to the buildings. Many Gothic churches have more area of glass than of walls; the clerestory of the choir in Amiens Cathedral, for example, has forty times more area of the void or window space than of the solid stone, and in some cases there are no walls, as in the highly scientific construction of the upper portion of the choir in the Cathedral of Prague, where all is glass set in the stone vaulting shafts. Other large churches or cathedrals built in the Gothic style might be given as illustrations where the proportion of void to solid is very great and consequently the windows are very large, such as Chartres, Cologne, Canterbury, Lincoln and York. In the smaller

Gothic churches of England, or on the Continent, this proportion of void to solid was generally reversed, and owing to this, and also to the greater use of wood in the roofs and screens, the smaller churches everywhere were at this time more richly treated in colour than the larger ones. The painter and decorator also found more employment in the treatment of secular buildings with coloured decoration in the Gothic period than he did on the cathedrals. It was only in rare instances that important wall paintings have been found in churches of this period; the colour and decoration, apart from the stained glass, was, especially in the case of the cathedrals, confined to mouldings, vault ribs, capitals, piers; and sometimes the webs, or ceilings of the vaults, were wholly filled with arabesque decoration, but often only partially so, around the bosses that marked the intersection of the ribs. (Plate 24.) It was in the smaller churches, and in the chambers and chapels attached to larger churches and cathedrals, in the crypts, sacristies, baptisteries, and sanctuaries, that complete schemes of colour decoration were carried out, or attempted in the Gothic period. It might be mentioned that some effective colour notes were obtained by the richly-coloured and gilt carvings and sculpture in wood and stone screens, altar-pieces, and the carved and painted tabernacles, which have been found in great numbers in the Gothic churches of Germany.

The stained-glass windows of the Gothic period, especially of the twelfth and thirteenth centuries, were the finest and best understood colour decoration in the glass material that has ever been done. Though many fine windows belonging to this time are found throughout Germany, Flanders, Bohemia, and Austria, the best examples are found in France, as at Chartres, and in England at York. The colouring of the glass of this period has never been surpassed for its splendour and beauty, and the figure-work and general ornamentation are designed and drawn in a suitably flat and architectonic style, in harmony with the material. The flat tapestry-like effect of the designs gives the work an appearance of mosaic in glass, and the result is what it should be, namely, a decorative work in "stained" glass, not "painted." In the fifteenth century and later, stained glass became degraded to the imitation of pictures, or light and shade paintings in glass, and consequently lost its legitimate character as a mosaic in glass. In a word, it became eventually pictorial in character, and ceased to have the true quality of stained glass. This later degradation of coloured glass was common to Germany, France, Italy and England.

The love for colour decoration, as applied to the interiors and exteriors of secular buildings and private dwellings, was more marked in Germany than in other European countries during the Middle Ages, and, as we would expect, Germany, with a tenacious and faithful conservatism, has clung more closely to her old traditional love for colour and decoration, and still takes a greater pride in all the circumstance of civic processions and pageantry, than any other nation in Europe. If we seek for an explanation of this we shall find that it is an inherited love from their ancestors, the old Germanic warriors and chiefs, who ruled the country before the days of Charlemagne, and who took a passionate delight in colour and in personal adornment. We may take one illustration of this artistic conservatism, among many others, by pointing out that the Germans paint and decorate their restaurants to-day, for example, in the same way as they did in the days of the fifteenth century.

Plate 24.—Decoration in Colour of a Groined Ceiling in the Church of St. Jacques, Liége, 1522-1588.

The museums of Cologne and Munich especially, contain many fragments of interior decorative painting that were taken from the old houses in their neighbourhoods. Such specimens of the old work are generally treated very flatly and only in a few colours, resembling tapestry designs, all of them having strong outlines that mark out the forms, like the constructive outline leads of window glass. We may point to one of the many fragments of this work which is now in the museum at Cologne: it consists of a portion of a deep and battlemented frieze, having three panels painted with scenes from the story of the Prodigal Son (*der lieblose Sohn*), and is executed in tempera in flat tints of reds, blues, pale yellows and greys, outlined in black. This frieze once formed a part of the decoration of the dining-hall *des Hauses Glesch auf der Hochstrasse*, Cologne.

Wooden panelled ceilings of private dwellings in the Gothic and Renaissance periods were strongly coloured, and the deep friezes on the walls were painted with figure subjects, heraldry, foliage, flowers and birds, or sometimes with conventional ornament alone, all the work being usually painted in tempera, while the walls below were either panelled with inlaid woods, or carved in wood or stone. In some cases the lower portion of the wall was painted on the wood or plaster, or hung with figured tapestries. It may be mentioned that the Germans have always made the greatest possible use of decorative heraldry, which was designed with great skill, in an elaborate and sumptuous manner, and used by them in every form and material of decorative art.

The adornment of the exteriors and interiors of their public buildings, and also of the better class of private houses, has always been a passion with the Germans. Many of the old houses in such cities as Lübeck, a northern German town of the Renaissance, Brunswick, Hildesheim, Frankfort, Strasburg, Nuremberg, Rothenburg, and the Swabian city of Augsburg are enriched with a wealth of carving and painting, of one or of both, on their façades, and in the interiors of their principal rooms, many examples of which are still in existence. The carving and painting in and on the houses of the Germans were in most cases designed and executed by native artists and craftsmen, but in some instances there are records of foreigners being employed, as in the case of the Fuggerhaus at Augsburg, where Hans Fugger, a member of that powerful and wealthy family, had his house decorated in the Italian Renaissance style, in 1570, the work being done by Italian artists.

The native love for decoration and colour has always been respected in Germany by the ruling powers, by the municipalities and wealthy citizens, who have always encouraged and fostered the decorative arts. The Germans take a civic pride in not only having handsome town-halls, theatres, railway stations, art galleries, museums, colleges, universities, and other public buildings, erected as the best possible examples of fine architecture, but in the adornment of such buildings with sculpture, fresco, mosaic and other colour decoration.

We might extend these observations on the colouring of architecture in Germany with a brief description of a few examples of modern work of the art which has engaged our attention.

The Teutonic love for the Gothic style and for its auxiliary colour and ornamentation is manifested in the decoration of almost every public building in modern Germany. This is even apparent in the fittings and decorations of the luxurious saloons of their great and latest-built passenger ships, where the dining-rooms and drawing-rooms of the modern liners are often, as in the case of the *Imperator*, designed and decorated in the style and true spirit of Medieval Gothic, so that the passengers might almost imagine that they were living in some castle or baronial hall of the fifteenth century instead of being on board the ship.

Plate 25.—Example of Diaper Ornament, largely used in Italian, German and English Decoration of the Sixteenth Century.

The staircase walls and ceiling of the Museum at Cologne present a fairly good scheme of modern German decoration. The walls have fresco paintings by Steinle, which are important examples of this modern German painter. The ornamentation that surrounds the frescoes, and that on the lower parts of the walls are not so good in colour or form as that of the vaulted ceiling. The work on the latter is good in colour and successfully carried out. The vaults have crimson-red, and blue background alternating, on which are painted a well-designed scroll-like ornamentation in lighter shades with some gold introduced on the mouldings and other parts, the whole effect being rich and pleasing.

Richly coloured carved wood ceilings, in low relief, which contain numerous heraldic shields arranged in panels, and set in suitable ornamentation of foliage forms and ribbon-work, are found in nearly all of the more important rooms in the German town-halls. One of the finest examples of a coloured and carved ceiling is the one which adorns the Kaiserhalle in the Römer, or town-hall, of Frankfort-on-the-Maine. This magnificent ceiling is carved in low-relief which gives it a suitable flat appearance. The rich tinctures of the charges on the shields, combined with the gold and silver that is used, produce, with the dark background of the natural brown colour of the wood, an extremely satisfactory example of refined decoration. This ceiling is certainly the best of its kind that we can remember to have seen in any German city. The walls of this magnificent chamber are decorated with good full-length portraits of the German and Prussian kings and emperors. At the entrance end of the hall there is a seated figure of Charlemagne, by Veit, and in the panel above is a wall painting by Steinle with the subject of "The Judgment of Solomon." The full-length portrait of Frederick I (1152-90), is an unusually fine work by Lessing.

Another example of a finely carved and painted ceiling, is that of the Council Chamber in the Rathaus, or town-hall at Hildesheim. Here also are seen the heraldic devices, with figures and elaborate scroll-work which compose the design of this ceiling. The general scheme of the colouring is rich and deep in tones of red, blue, gold, on the background of dark brown wood. The walls of this Gothic chamber are decorated with fine paintings in fresco by H. Prell, begun in 1892. With the exception of there being too much darkness in some parts, they are otherwise brilliant and luminous in colour, and may be said to be among the best examples of fresco technique in Germany.

The interior of the town-hall at Aix-la-Chapelle is admirably decorated, and in a similar manner to those of Hildesheim and Frankfort. The Coronation Chamber in this building contains the celebrated historical fresco paintings by Alfred Rethel, four of which were painted by this artist, and the other four were designed by Rethel, but painted by Professor Kehren. The vaulted ceilings and piers are richly decorated in colour, and windows with stained glass.

The principal staircase walls of the New Museum in Berlin are decorated with six great frescoes by Kaulbach, representing certain epochs in the history of mankind. These wall paintings are executed in the water-glass method of fresco. As wall decorations they are too pictorial in design, and the treatment, in the matter of colouring and technique, lacks simplicity. They are over-modelled in their light and shade, and the colouring presents too many violent contrasts, which greatly injures their value as monumental examples of legitimate wall decoration. Wherever white or light yellows occur in the work, these parts of the painting have evidently become disintegrated, and at present show a disagreeable chalkiness or bloom. This, together with the presence of many black and heavy shadows, which appear to have gone darker, if possible, with age, combine to throw the painting out of tone. In composition and drawing they are not without grandeur of style, but if they had been more simple in treatment, and less violent in colour and light and shade effects, they would be more pleasing as wall decorations.

In the Hall of the Gods, and in the two adjoining rooms on either side of the small vestibule in the Glyptothek at Munich there are some important frescoes by Cornelius, painted in 1820-30. The subjects of these paintings are classical, and represent the Abode of the Gods, the Legend of Prometheus, and the Trojan wars, all painted in rich and brilliant schemes of colour, but bordering on harshness. There is a great deal of auxiliary decoration in these rooms consisting of good examples of ornamentation in the Greco-Roman style of Grottesche in painting and in stucco-reliefs. The new Town-hall of Munich is well decorated with wall paintings, ornament, and heraldic work. The Council Chamber has a very large wall painting executed in oil on canvas by Piloty. The subject is an Allegorical History of Munich, and the magistrates' room has paintings by Lindenschmit and is also adorned with a finely carved and painted ceiling.

One of the finest schemes of modern German decoration is that of the great staircase of the Albertinum Sculpture Gallery at Dresden. The frescoes, by H. Prell, on the ceiling and walls have subjects of Greek mythology and are painted in bright and light schemes of colour, the general effect being very luminous, and the work is vigorous in execution. The dado and lower stonework has panels of bronze with low-relief decoration, and in the corridor of the landing there are some fine panels in mosaic.

Fresco, mosaic, tiles, and coloured marble have frequently been used, as the means of obtaining colour decoration on the exteriors of many public buildings in Germany, in modern times. On the upper part of the façade of the Kunst-Gewerbe Museum at Berlin there are a fine series of square-shaped panels containing mosaics in colour on gold grounds, designed by Professor Ewald, and by Geselchap.

The exterior wall of the Royal Historical Museum at Dresden has an important decoration, consisting of a long and deep frieze, executed in a light yellow stone-colour and black on a gold-coloured ground. The material is a kind of porcelain or tile composition, having a sgraffito-like treatment. The work was made in the Royal Porcelain Manufactory at Meissen. The subject of this frieze is a procession of kings and warriors of Saxony on horseback who ruled from 1170 to 1873, and who are represented in chronological order.

There are many buildings in Germany that have had their exteriors decorated with paintings in fresco, but much of this work is now in a decayed condition. Many modern houses, such as restaurants and shops, have exterior decorations painted in oil. The outside walls of the Old (Alt) Museum at Berlin have an extensive arrangement of panels painted in fresco, having mythological subjects, such as the Labours of Hercules, etc., but they are now in a dirty and faded condition. As an example of exterior colouring we might mention the beautiful Gothic fountain, the Schöne Brunnen, erected about 1360, in the market place of Nuremberg. This fountain is built in the shape of a pyramid, in a rich Gothic style; it has, however, been restored several times. It is decorated with many figures of kings, prophets, apostles, and other worthies, and is always kept painted in its original colouring of blue, red, and gold.

We may conclude this review of German coloured decoration of buildings by a brief notice of some of the painted wood and stone carvings which are found plentifully in old German churches, and more particularly in those of Nuremberg. The Church of St. Lawrence at Nuremberg contains several examples of carved wood altar-pieces in the form of triptychs, the centre panels of which are carved with scriptural subjects, the figures being in high relief and painted in rich colours, in order to harmonise with the colour of the two painted leaves on either side of it. Hanging from the roof in the centre of this church is the celebrated circular wood carving by Veit Stoss, all richly coloured and gilt. It consists of a representation of the Annunciation, and the surrounding circular frame is of a beautiful design of open work ornamented with roses, and with seven medallions with representations of the Seven Joys of the Virgin. In this church there is also a very interesting fourteenth-century altar-piece in Gothic stone-carving which is erected in a bay on the left of the east end of the church. It is a good example of the colouring of the period, and is painted in tints of yellowish-red and warm green, with a soft dull blue in the background parts, and the salient points and narrow mouldings are gilt. On many of the structural parts and mouldings of this Church there are still remains of the fourteenth and fifteenth century colouring. Remains of similar colouring are found in many parts of the Church of St. Sebaldus, at Nuremberg, more particularly on the ribs of the vaults, piers, and ceilings, etc. In this church may be seen the celebrated Crucifixion with the figures of the Saviour, the Virgin, and St. John, in carved wood and richly coloured, which is the work of Veit Stoss (1520). Another example of painted and gilded wood carving in this church is the statue of the Madonna (1450) under a canopy of Gothic design.

Plate 26.—Example of Diaper Pattern, used in Italian, German
and English Decoration of the Sixteenth Century.

Plate 27.—Example of Diaper Ornament, used in Italian, German and English Decoration of the Sixteenth Century.

CHAPTER IX
COLOUR DECORATION IN ENGLAND

THE polychromatic decoration of buildings in England, like the architecture, was in a great measure a development of, or at least was strongly influenced in its inception by, Italian and French art; we might add, also by German and Flemish decorative art of the fourteenth and fifteenth centuries.

It may be said that English decorative art and colouring has, and always had, a certain style and character of its own which has distinguished it from that of other countries, but we must admit that the seeds from whence it sprang were not all of native origin. The English tree of art was not indigenous to the country, but rather an exotic that grew extremely well after it became deeply rooted in the receptive and fertile soil of England. If this be true of the historical beginnings of British art, it must also be said, on the other hand, that the original features and complexion of the adopted art have been completely changed to an aspect of British nativeness.

The brief outlines, given in the previous chapters, of the practice of coloured decoration in Italy, France, and Germany may throw some light on the styles and methods of ornamental design and colouring as practised in our own countries, especially in medieval times.

In the pre-Norman days English churches were decorated in colour, though in a rude manner. The Venerable Bede relates that in the year 678 the Monastery of Weremouth was decorated with paintings done by French artists. Paintings and tapestry hangings were the usual adornment of the pre-Norman churches. As early as 674 Wilfrid, Bishop of York, had the walls, the sacrium arch, and capitals of the columns of his church decorated with sacred subjects, and otherwise richly coloured.

Nothing, however, except a few traces of colour on some very old edifices now exists that dates from the period anterior to Norman times, and even only a little of the colouring on mouldings, carvings, and other portions of the Norman architecture of our great cathedrals and smaller churches, but such portions of colouring as still remain are sufficient to prove that the buildings of the Norman period, in common with all pre-Reformation churches, must have been decorated and coloured from floor to ceiling.

The colours used were very few and simple, such as red, black, and yellow only in some schemes, but in others, blues and greens were introduced.

Mural paintings and sacred subjects, together with the subordinate ornamental decoration, once covered the interiors of Norman churches, but little traces are now left of such. Decorative patterns in simulation of Norman mouldings and diapers were still used in the decoration of later churches up to the end of the first quarter of the thirteenth century.

Frequent mention of colour decoration in England is made in the records, or Close Rolls, of Henry III, dating from the first decade of the thirteenth century. In these documents we find references to the painting of the king's chambers in his palaces at Westminster, Guilford, Windsor, Winchester, and Clarendon, and mention is made of certain colours and gold, as well as of oil and varnish. References are also made to the making of stained-glass windows; and we know that miniature painting was practised in England at that period. The subject-pictures and ornamentation of the illuminated manuscripts were often copied on the walls of churches and palaces, and also in stained-glass windows of this time.

This English king had a great passion for adorning his numerous palaces and chapels with painted decoration and stained-glass. He also encouraged the art of miniature painting, and, to mention one instance of this, he ordered a large book of miniatures, which contained the illustrations and record of the exploits of his heroic uncle, King Richard I, at the siege of Antioch during the Crusade. It is also mentioned that he "ordered that the exploits should be the subjects of paintings on the wainscot of a room in the royal palace at Clarendon." These "exploits" also formed the subjects of other paintings that were executed fourteen years later in the Tower of London, and also in the Antioch (Jews') Chamber at Westminster. One curious and intimate connection with the painting of miniatures, as book-illustrations and mural painting, is shown by the circumstance of the king's librarian being also the custodian of the colours, which he supplied to the decorators by order of the king. It is evident from this that colours used for the illumination of books and for wall-paintings were possibly of the same kind, and perhaps of the same value.

In some old illuminated manuscripts there are frequently representations of interiors of rooms having various decorative patterns on the painted walls and ceilings, and in some cases they are painted as "Stellari Aureo," set with stars of gold, on a blue or green ground. In connection with this it is interesting to find that the first mention of a Star Chamber occurs in the Roll of Liveries of Henry III, in these words: "Precept to the Sheriff of Southampton that he cause the Chamber at Winchester to be painted of a green colour, and with stars of gold (*and compartments or panels*) in which may be painted histories from the Old and New Testaments."

That the colour decoration of interiors was common, even before the time of Henry III, appears so from another precept issued by the king to the effect that the wainscot in the king's chamber in the castle at Winchester is "to be painted with the same pictures as formerly."

Some native painters were employed by Henry III, as the names of at least two are mentioned—Edward of Westminster and Master Walter—but the Italian, "William of Florence," the monk of Westminster, seems to have been the principal painter and decorator-in-chief to the king, for, as a rule, the native artists and decorators carried out the work under his direction and supervision.

At this time, and even later, up to the end of the seventeenth century, many Italian, French, and Flemish artists were invited to this country by the English king, and many others were attracted to England owing to the demand for decorated work. Although there were a good number of native artists and decorators working throughout the country, there were also a considerable number of foreign artists who, generally speaking, belonged to some of the religious orders, and who travelled about and decorated many churches and secular edifices in England. It may be mentioned that much of the artistic decoration, painted by the foreign artist-monks, consisted of copies of miniature paintings from illuminated manuscripts.

The great immigration of these foreign painters, decorators, and stained-glass craftsmen, in the fourteenth and fifteenth centuries, served to arouse a healthy competition between themselves and the native English decorators and craftsmen, and a great improvement took place in the work of the native artists, although the best work has generally been ascribed to the foreign painters.

It is difficult to realise to what extent the churches and secular buildings were coloured and decorated in the centuries named in England; but we have sufficient proofs from the remains of the colouring that still exists, as well as from documentary evidence, that the walls, ceilings, piers, arches, capitals and mouldings of church interiors, whether the materials were of stone, wood, or plaster, were all richly coloured and gilt, so that from floor to roof the churches of medieval England glowed in schemes of solemn splendour of colour and gold, the whole effect being assisted by the additional colour harmony of the stained glass windows.

At the present time the interiors of most of these old churches are bereft of their former glory of colour, this being due to centuries of neglect, and perhaps vandalism. Some of them have, certainly, a spotty bit of colour and decoration at the east end, and occasionally a few coloured glass windows. It is only in a rare instance that one of these old churches is treated anew in a full and finished scheme of decorated colouring; the majority still keep to their fashionable whitewash, with a few spots of colour dotted about; their former beauty has ceased to remain to them, and nobody at present seems interested enough to make a serious attempt to bring it back.

Some critics strongly assert and argue that these old churches and other ancient edifices should not be restored, either to the former glory of coloured decoration or in their structural features. One critic follows another by repeating the arguments of his predecessor in art criticism, namely, that old buildings should be permitted to crumble slowly into decay, ruin, and nothingness, and also, that you cannot restore anything that does not exist. These arguments would appear logical enough when applied to the case of structures that are already so far ruined that they cannot be used for the purposes for which they were built, but if an edifice, though hoary with age and weather-worn by stress and storm, is yet sufficiently solid and sound to be used, as in the early days of its prime and beauty, there is absolutely no reason why it should not be carefully and lovingly restored, or repaired where necessary, both in its structural parts and in its colour decoration, so long as it can still be used for the performance of the duties or the fulfilment of such functions as those to which it was originally dedicated.

The best examples of coloured decoration in England, of the fourteenth and fifteenth centuries, is found in the East Anglian churches, chiefly in the counties of Norfolk and Suffolk, though in the west and southern midland counties the decoration of churches received great attention at this time, but it was inferior to the work done in East Anglia. Several reasons to account for this superiority of the East Anglian art have been given, the principal one being that at the time of the greatest activity in church decoration in the eastern counties, these parts of the country were in a very prosperous condition, owing to the flourishing state of their cloth and wool trade, and the close connection of East Anglia in intercourse and trade with Flanders. In the fourteenth century Edward III, in 1328, brought over many Flemish weavers to Norfolk, and during the following century and afterwards many Flemish and German painters and decorators doubtless came across to this part of England, and obtained employment in the decoration of churches.

It has also been suggested that the superior quality and quantity of decorative painting in East Anglia was due to the greater use of wood for church fittings, especially oak, in this part of the country, and the scarcity of stone. There was a cheap and plentiful supply of wood in Norfolk and Suffolk, but the only kind of stone was flint, of which the churches were mostly built. Wood, therefore, and the plastered walls, suggested painting, more so than stone, which was more used in the building of churches in other parts of England. Accordingly we find that the rood-screens, and other timber fittings of the East Anglian churches, were all elaborately coloured, and painted with figures and decorative patterns. (Plates 4, 25, 27, 28.)

Flemish painting at that time had attained to great excellence, and there is no doubt that it strongly influenced the English art of the fifteenth century, and especially the decorative school of art which about that time rose to great eminence in East Anglia. Flemish methods and styles of church colouring and painting, and especially that of the rood-screens, roofs and reredoses, were freely adopted by the English decorative artists, and the types of the painted figures of saints, prophets and apostles, as well as the style and character of the floral and geometric ornamentation, which has been found in the existing decoration of the old English churches, had all their counterparts in Flemish church decoration (Plate 24). The best examples of the English work of this period that are still in existence are the rood-screens of Norfolk, particularly those of Ranworth (Plates 4 and 28), Barton Turf, Aylsham, and Cawston, and the screens of Southwold church in Suffolk. The painting on these screens is decidedly English in character and technique, however much the designs of the single figures may be Flemish or German in style.

From a Water-Colour by W. Davidson

Plate 28.—Saint George. From the Rood Screen, Ranworth Church, Norfolk: Early Sixteenth Century. From a Water-colour by W. Davidson, Architect.

[From a Drawing by W. Davidson.

Plate 29.—Decorated Mouldings, from the Rood Screen, Marsham Church, Norfolk: English, Sixteenth Century. Drawn by W. Davidson.

The interior wall surfaces of the smaller English churches were usually coated with plaster, while the walls of the large ones and those of the cathedrals were of smooth-faced stone. The plaster surface was prepared for painting by simply coating it with a light, cream coloured, or pale grey wash of distemper. The decorative patterns and emblematic devices were painted on these grounds, or on similarly prepared grounds of soft-coloured tints of red, blue, or green. The patterns were sometimes painted in one colour only, but often in two or three, one of which being gold, or yellow, to imitate the colour of gold. On white, grey, or cream-coloured grounds the tints were usually dark grey, red, black, or green, and on the brighter colored grounds the pattern colours were generally in grey or black, or in a darker tint of the colour of the ground.

Although the early English decorators were good colorists, the range of the colour was limited, but they made good use of the small number of the colours they employed by often cleverly transposing and alternating the grouping or arrangements, so that although the same colour on the same pattern might be used, the transposition by alternation of the pattern gave great interest and variety to the general scheme of colour. Reds, yellows, black and white were the principal colours used in the early Gothic decoration; blues, greens and gold were added to these in the later periods, especially in the decoration and figure paintings on the rood-screens and ceilings, and on the woodwork generally.

Mouldings, whether of wood or stone were always coloured, as well as the piers, capitals and columns; the oak woodwork was invariably painted, as oak was cheap and common in those days, and the natural grain of the wood was evidently not much prized.

Mistakes were, of course, sometimes made by the early English decorators in their over-zealous application of colour, when, for example, they painted over some of the finest workmanship in carved stone as well as some of the costly materials. As instances of such mistakes, it may be mentioned that the black marble shafts in the choir of Rochester Cathedral showed traces of their having been at one time painted red; the beautiful white marble monument of Archbishop Walter Gray in York Minster was at one time painted in various colours, and the shrine of St. Alban, in St. Alban's Cathedral, though of Purbeck marble, is painted blue and green, the traceries and mullions being gilded.

The character and motives of the decorative patterns were interesting and diversified. A common treatment of the wall spaces between bands, and panels which contained pictorial decoration, consisted in the painting of a simple masonry pattern where double lines of red or yellow were drawn horizontally and vertically, so as to form rectangular spaces which corresponded to the joints of the wall, and in the centre of each oblong there was usually placed a circular flower form. Diapers and checkered patterns were used very much to fill wall spaces and panelling. The diapers were sometimes sparsely arranged, when they would then appear as sprig-like forms, "powdered," or "sprinkled" at regulated intervals: these were known as "open" diapers; but when the diaper forms were more elaborate and important, and fitted closer together, they were called "close" diapers. The latter variety of diaper pattern was generally copied from the elaborate designs which decorated the rich Florentine and Sicilian silks of woven damask. These damask silks were used as hangings and for sumptuous dress materials, and may be seen represented as such in many of the Italian and Flemish paintings of the fourteenth and fifteenth and sixteenth centuries. Examples of the open diapers or powderings may be seen on the backgrounds of the panel paintings on the East Anglian screens, and the more elaborate, close diapers appear on the richly decorated dresses of the figures (Plates 4, 25-27, 28).

[From a Drawing by W. Davidson.

Plate 30.—Decorated Mouldings, from the Rood Screen, Cawston Church, Norfolk: English, Early Sixteenth Century. Drawn by W. Davidson.

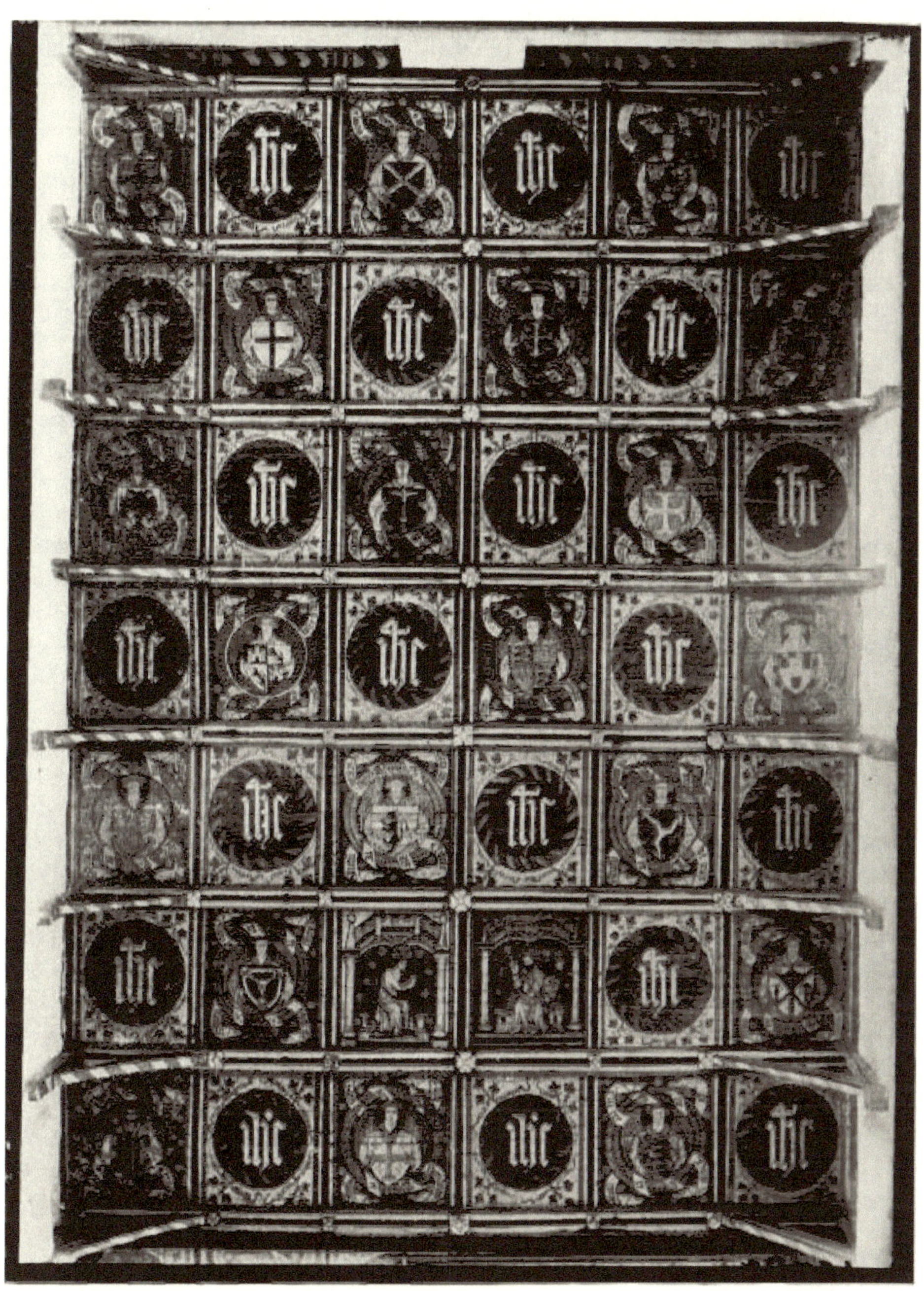

Plate 31.—Portion of Ceiling Decoration, Choir of St. Albans Abbey.

In the latter important class of diaper the pattern is often made up of such details as conventional animals, birds, flowers, foliage, ornament and fruit, such as the pomegranate and pine-apple, all cleverly arranged to make repeating patterns, these patterns being later developments of those found in the older Siculo-Arabian silks and Byzantine silk tapestries (Plates 25-27), hence the oriental character of this class of ornament.

Various devices, heraldic and otherwise, and emblems, were sometimes superimposed over the central parts of diapered walls and ceilings, and painted in different colours or in gold. Mottoes, texts in ornamental lettering on scrolls, and monograms, very much repeated, were all used as decorative motives, and also flat representations of architectural forms, especially of Gothic tracery. Lead stars, wavy-rayed, and gilded, were fastened to ceilings that were painted blue, thus giving a conventional representation of the firmament.

Projecting mouldings of windows and doorways, and arches, and the ribs of groined ceilings of the old churches, were all painted in parti-colours, and the fillets were usually gilded. It was a common practice to colour the groined and flat ceiling ribs and mouldings only a short distance from the bosses which decorated their intersections, and also a similar portion of the web, or ceiling portion around the bosses, but often the whole of the ribs and ceiling panels were richly decorated in colours, and with elaborate patterns of diapered work or arabesques. Stone and carved wood bosses were usually gilded, and the interstices behind the carved foliage, masks, or figures on them, were painted in some very strong colour, usually red, in order to relieve the carving. As a rule carved enrichments were either gilded or painted yellow to represent gold.

In this period of great activity in church decoration in England special attention was given to the painting of roofs with their rafters and beams. St. Alban's Abbey (Plate 31), Blythburgh in Suffolk, Sall Church in Norfolk, Plymouth Cathedral, Ufford Church, near Ipswich, and numerous others had all richly-painted roofs, although the generality of roofs were simple in colouring, most of them having red, black and grey decorations painted on a white or a blue ground. Sometimes, however, the ceiling decoration was more elaborate, as we have already seen, when it consisted of rich scroll-work, interspersed with emblems, monograms and various devices. Tracery patterns, flower and leaf designs decorated the rafters, and the round bead mouldings were often treated in spiral twistings of lines or patterns, like strips of ribbon round a rod, this kind of treatment being known as "barber-poling."

Much of the pattern decoration of the old churches had somewhat the appearance of stencilling, which might be accounted for by the flat character of the designs. The painted decoration was, however, not stencilled, but was first applied to the surfaces by the method known as "pouncing," by means of the pricked holes made in the original tracing or drawing, and the pattern work afterwards executed with the brush. That this method was adopted is proved by the slight variation in the drawing of the painted patterns, and by the characteristic freedom in the execution which brushwork can only give, and further by the absence of the effect which is due to "ties" of the stencil-plate. In some instances the oft-recurring rosettes and diaper powderings may have been stencilled as an easy and preliminary method of placing them in their regular positions, but if so, they were afterwards finished with the brush, by hand, as they have nothing of the appearance of patterns produced by stencil printing.

Plate 32.—Decoration on the Rood Screen, Ranworth Church, Norfolk: Early Sixteenth Century. Drawn by W. Davidson.

The materials and mediums used in the painting of walls, ceilings, or woodwork, were the dry colours ground in water, and mixed with parchment or egg size. The latter size, with or without the addition of fig-tree juice, was chiefly used in the painting of the figure subjects and pictorial work, while size made from cuttings of parchment, by boiling them, or from ordinary glue, was used for the larger surface colouring. The general medium of the work was therefore tempera, or distemper, though sometimes, but rarely, oil was mixed with the colours. Pictorial and ornamental paintings on the screens were varnished with an oil varnish over the tempera painting, but in many instances such paintings were left unvarnished. Most, if not all, of the decoration on the screens, pulpits, and the woodwork generally, in the English medieval churches, was certainly executed in tempera, with the egg-size medium, which was the common method of picture or panel painting on the Continent at that time, and most of the pictorial decorations were varnished afterwards, so that those which remain to this day have the appearance of oil paintings, and this has led many to class them wrongly as such.

The subjects on the screens, pulpits and reredoses were generally representations of saints, apostles, prophets, kings, queens, knights and angels, etc. The figures were usually placed on alternate red and green grounds, the latter being diapered over in small patterns in white, purple, or gold. In some cases a raised gesso diapered ground of gold has been prepared, as in the Southwold screens. The robes of the figures were also richly decorated with elaborate patterns, in colours heightened with gold.

There are still some remains of decorative painting on the screens of many medieval churches in Devon and Cornwall, but as a rule the work on these screens does not possess so high an artistic value as that of the East Anglian painting. In Devon most of the screens are found in churches between Totnes and Exeter. The best examples are those at Ashton, Plymtree, Buckland-in-the-Moor, Wellcombe, and the miniature-like paintings at Hennock on the hill above the Teign valley. Some painted screens in Devon of a later date, at Southpool, Blackawton, and Chivelston, are the only ones, according to Father Camm, out of forty in Devonshire that contain fillings of arabesque ornament, all the rest having painted figures. The ornament on these is in the Italian Renaissance style, with the Elizabethan English influence. The colouring of these arabesques is white, on grounds of red and green.

We have treated the subject of medieval colour decoration in England at some length, but our excuse for this must be that the period it embraces was one of the greatest activity in the history of decorative art in this country. Further, it may be said, it was in this time that churches and other buildings were coloured completely throughout, and not as in the more modern custom, where, with a few exceptions, churches and secular buildings are treated with a few isolated bits of colour, which being also done at different times, and by different hands, cannot possibly have any sort of homogeneity or unity as a suitable colour finish for the building. When any of us are fortunate enough to be trusted, or favoured with an opportunity to decorate the interior of a building completely throughout, we might do worse—we cannot do better—than take some lessons from the practice and methods adopted and followed out so successfully by the early English decorators.

Though little now remains of this old coloured decoration, that little enables us to construct from the fragments the scheme and colour of the entire work, as the anatomist is able to construct a prehistoric creation from the skeleton, or even from a portion of it.

During the seventeenth and eighteenth centuries colour decoration of buildings was almost non-existent in England, for interiors that showed any pretension to decoration were finished, or unfinished, in schemes of white and gold. Sometimes, however, the decorator was permitted to revel in pale shades of pea-green, "French grey," very pale blues and still paler pinks, so that many interiors of the Adam and Georgian styles, though famous for their delicate ornamentation in stucco plaster work, were either left white, like brides' cake decoration, or in the pale tints of other kinds of sugar confectionery, a dainty, but timid type of colour decoration which we borrowed from France (Plate 33).

About the latter half of the eighteenth century, after the discovery of Pompeii, in 1753, with its richly-coloured wall decoration, colour began to show itself on the interior walls and ceilings of some English buildings, both of a public and private nature, but not in churches, for it was not until about the middle of the nineteenth century that there was a partial revival of church decoration, a sort of renaissance of the fourteenth and fifteenth century work, that was brought about chiefly by Pugin, Sir Gilbert Scott, and other neo-Gothic architects. Many churches were decorated in England about this time in schemes of rich and strong colouring, and with similar types of ornament to those used by the early English decorators. Two very elaborately-coloured and decorated examples may be mentioned, namely, the chapel or crypt at Westminster Houses of Parliament, and that of the Catholic Church at Cheadle, in Staffordshire, after Pugin's designs. The colour decorations of these two churches are among the rare examples of Gothic colour revival, where the interiors have been finished in complete schemes of strong colouring.

During the last fifty years there have been many fine examples of hall decoration painted in fresco in England, as well as important pictorial and ornamental schemes of decoration in coloured plaster, mosaic, and in oil painting. We might mention the Houses of Parliament frescoes, those at South Kensington, the Royal Exchange wall pictures, the mosaics in St. Paul's Cathedral, and in the new Cathedral at Westminster, as well as a good deal of coloured decoration in private houses and civic buildings throughout the country, but in the British Isles the advancement of this interesting and fascinating art is severely handicapped by the indifference, prejudice and obstinacy, even of many people who profess to have a love for art.

As a nation, we are a long way behind the French, Germans and Americans in the encouragement of decorative art. The Governments and municipalities of Germany and France decorate their civic and public buildings thoroughly, and with no niggard hand, but in our own countries such work, however good it may be, is commissioned for in a partial and piecemeal way, when it is decided to be done at all.

Plate 33.—Portion of Room Decoration formerly existing at Sheen House, Surrey. Eighteenth Century.

Plate 34.—Portion of Staircase Decoration in the Victoria and Albert Museum.
By F. W. Moody.

INDEX

Symbols

Ægina *54*

A

Aix-la-Chapelle *62, 70*
Albertinum Sculpture Gallery *71*
Alfred Norman *57*
Alfred Rethel *70*
Amiens *61, 65*
Arabesques *19, 25, 35, 47, 49, 51, 84, 86*
Artificial Light *14, 36, 37*
Assisi *42, 43*
Augsburg *68*

B

Bartolomeo *27*
Baths of Diocletian *47*
Belgium *26*
Bellini *49*
Berlin *70, 71*
Bishop of York *75*
Blake *61*
Borgia Apartments *19*
Botticelli *43, 61*
Brunswick Cathedral *64*
Burne-Jones *6*
Byzantine decoration *51*
Byzantine mosaicists *31*

C

Cairo *57*
Camerini *49*
Capitol *63, 64*
Cardinal Richelieu *49*
Cassoni *43*

Cawston Church *82*
Charlemagne *62, 66, 70*
Charles Garnier *57*
Church of St. Gereon *63, 64*
Church of St. John *40, 41, 42*
Church of St. Lawrence *72*
Church of St. Sebaldus *72*
Cimabue *38, 42*
Close Rolls *76*
Cluny Museum *53*
Coliseum *47*
Cologne *63, 64, 65, 67, 68, 70*
Colour Decoration *vi, 1, 2, 3, 5, 27, 53, 56, 57, 59, 62, 63, 65, 66, 68, 71, 75, 76, 78, 86, 87*
Coloured marbles *5, 25, 28*
Coloured materials *12, 26, 57*
Colour treatment *14, 20, 30, 31*
Contours *20, 30, 34, 35*
Cornelius *71*
Cornices *12, 31, 42, 58*
Costa *49*
Cottages *2*
Cour-du-Murier *57*
Cristoforo Romano *49*
Cromwell *2, 3*
C. Rosselli *43*
Curved surfaces *17*

D

Dado *14, 22, 24, 71*
Deck *58*
Decorators of primitive Greece *28*
Denuelle *57*
Detaille *60*
Didron *54*
Doge's Palace *26*
Dresden *71*
Duban *57*
Ducal Palace *27, 47, 48, 49, 51*

E

École de Mosaïque *58*
École des Beaux-Arts *57*
Edward of Westminster *76*
E. Hébert *58*

Exterior colouring *5, 26, 72*
Exteriors of buildings *5, 26, 53, 54*

F

Flat ceiling *17, 19, 43, 65, 84*
Flat ceilings *19*
Florence *19, 26, 42, 43, 45, 49*
Fontainebleau *50, 54*
France *vi, 27, 31, 38, 53, 54, 56, 57, 58, 59, 66, 75, 87*
François I *50, 53*
Frankfort *68, 70*
Frescoes of Giotto *43*
Fresco paintings *26, 70*
Frieze decoration *22, 23*
Frodoard *53*
Fuggerhaus *68*

G

Galerie-du-Louvre *57*
Galland *59*
Gallo-Roman era *53*
G. Boni *27*
Genoa *19*
Germany *vi, 26, 27, 38, 54, 62, 64, 65, 66, 68, 70, 71, 75, 87*
Gerspach *58*
Geselchap *71*
Ghirlandaio *19*
Giotto *39, 42, 47*
Giovanni Buon *27*
Giovanni da Udine *19, 47, 49*
Giulio Romano *19, 46, 47, 48, 49, 50, 51*
Gonzaga *49*
Gothic decoration *44, 81*
Gothic glass *30*
Gothic period *64, 65, 66*
Greece *54*
Greek polychromy *54*
Greek temples *11, 54*
Gregory of Tours *53*
Grottesche *47, 51, 71*

H

Hampton Court *3*
Henri II *53*
Henry III *76*

Hildesheim *65, 68, 70*
Hippolyte Flandrin *57*
Hittorf *54*
Holland *26*
Hospital of the Innocents *26*
Hôtel de Ville *60*
Houses of Parliament *87*
H. Prell *70, 71*

I

Interiors *12*
International Exhibitions *58*
Ipswich *84*
Isabella d'Este *49*
Italian decorative art *38*
Italian painted ceilings *19*
Italian Primitive School *59*
Italian Renaissance *19, 38, 56, 68, 86*

K

Kaulbach *70*
Kehren *70*
Kleinkünste *62*

L

Labrouste *57*
Lateran *40, 41, 42*
Lessing *70*
Lindenschmit *71*
Lorenzo *49*
Louis XIII *53*
Louis XIV *53*
Louvre *49*
Lübeck *68*

M

Maggiore *38*
Majolica dishes *43*
Mantegna *49*
Mantua *46, 47, 48, 49, 50, 51*
Marino Contarini *27*
Marquis Giovanni Francesco *49*
Master Walter *76*
Materials *5, 25, 27, 28, 58, 77, 81, 82, 85*

Michel Angelo *19, 22*
Middle Ages *9, 11, 53, 54, 57, 62, 66*
Milan *4, 26, 39*
Mohammedan palaces *57*
Monastery of San Marco *43*
Monastery of Weremouth *75*
Monument of Archbishop Walter Gray *81*
Mosaics *1, 2, 6, 11, 28, 38, 42, 57, 58, 59, 62, 71, 87*
Mosaic workers *58*
Mouldings *8, 12, 17, 19, 20, 21, 22, 24, 26, 27, 31, 33, 47, 51, 53, 58, 61, 63, 66, 70, 72, 75, 76, 77, 80, 81, 82, 84*
Munich *67, 71*

N

Napoleon *54, 57*
New Cathedral *11, 87*
New Museum *70*
Niccolo dell' Abbate *50, 51*
Norfolk *10, 21, 78, 79, 80, 82, 84, 85*
Norman period *75*
Notre Dame *53*
Nuremberg *68, 72*

O

Old house *43*
Opera House *57, 58*
Opus Alexandrinum *25*
Opus Sectile *25*

P

Palace of Titus *47*
Palaces at Mantua *19*
Palazza del Tè *51*
Palazzo Publico *42*
Palazzo Vecchio *19, 42, 46, 49*
Palladio *5*
Panthéon *58, 59, 60*
Paperhangings *16, 17*
Paradiso *49*
Paris *49, 53, 57, 58, 59, 60*
Parthenon *11, 22*
Paul Baudry *58*
Paul Sédille *58*
Paul Veronese *19, 59*
Perino del Vaga *19*

Perugia *19*
Perugino *19, 43, 49*
Piloty *71*
Pinturrichio *19, 43*
Plain surface *22*
Plain surfaces *12*
Plymouth Cathedral *84*
Poitiers *53*
Pompeii *28, 57, 87*
Pope Leo *47*
Pouncing *84*
Primaticcio *50, 51, 53*
Prince Vincenzo *49*
Professor Ewald *71*
Prosper Merimée *54*
Public buildings *vi, 3, 15, 26, 53, 61, 68, 71, 87*
Pugin *87*
Puvis de Chavannes *59, 60, 61*

R

Raffaelle *3, 19, 47, 48, 50, 51*
Ranworth Church *10, 21, 79, 85*
Rathaus *70*
Ravenna *59, 62*
Renaissance period *50, 53*
Revival of colour decoration *27, 54*
Richard I *76*
Rinaldo of Mantua *51*
Rochester Cathedral *81*
Romanesque and Gothic *23, 42*
Romanesque epoch in Germany *62*
Romanesque period *62, 63, 64, 65*
Romantic School *54*
Rome *19, 28, 38, 40, 41, 47, 48, 62*
Römer *70*
Rood-screens *9, 23, 78, 81*
Royal Exchange *87*
Royal Historical Museum *71*
Rubens *59*
Ruskin *1, 20*

S

Sainte Chapelle *57*
Sainte Geneviève *58*
Sala di Cambio *19*

Sala Piccolomini 19
Sall Church 84
Salle des Beaux-Arts 58
Salviati 62
San Clemente 38
San Pietro 47
Santa Maria del Popolo 19
Santa Maria Maggiore 19
Schöne Brunnen 72
Serlio 50, 53
Siena 19, 42, 43
Sir Gilbert Scott 87
Sistine Chapel 19, 22, 43
Small interval 32, 33
Southwold church 78
Spello 19
Staffordshire 87
Stained glass 1, 5, 9, 11, 35, 66, 70, 77
Steinle 64, 70
St. Michael's Church 65
Stoss 72

T

Temple of Empedocles 54
Temple of Jupiter 54
Theatres 14, 68
Tile decoration 2, 57
Tintoretto 19, 59
Titian 59
Torriti 38, 40, 42, 47
Town-hall 70, 71
Treatment of Walls 13

U

Ufford Church 84
Use of gold 31

V

Vasari 47, 49
Vatican Loggie 47, 49
Veit 70, 72
Venerable Bede 75
Venetian glass 44
Venice 19, 26, 27, 28, 62
Verona 26, 27, 44

Victor Baltard 57
Victoria and Albert Museum *vi, 34, 39, 45, 49, 54, 55, 56, 89*
Villa Madama *19, 47, 48*
Viollet-le-Duc *53, 54, 57*

W

Wainscoting *22*
Wellcombe *86*
Westminster *11, 76, 87*
Wilfrid *75*
William of Florence *76*
Wooden ceilings *23*

Lector House believes that a society develops through a two-fold approach of continuous learning and adaptation, which is derived from the study of classic literary works spread across the historic timeline of literature records. Therefore, we aim at reviving, repairing and redeveloping all those inaccessible or damaged but historically as well as culturally important literature across subjects so that the future generations may have an opportunity to study and learn from past works to embark upon a journey of creating a better future.

This book is a result of an effort made by Lector House towards making a contribution to the preservation and repair of original ancient works which might hold historical significance to the approach of continuous learning across subjects.

HAPPY READING & LEARNING!

LECTOR HOUSE LLP
E-MAIL: lectorpublishing@gmail.com